||| ||||| ||| |||| |||| ||| |||| ||| |||| |||
☑ **W9-BPK-396**

LACenter
F
869
.L89
N53
1997

DISCARDED
No Longer
APU
Property

AZUSA PACIFIC UNIVERSITY LIBRARIES
AZUSA. CALIFORNIA 91702-7000

UNDOCUMENTED IN L.A.

UNDOCUMENTED IN L.A.

An Immigrant's Story

DIANNE WALTA HART

A Scholarly Resources Inc. Imprint
Wilmington, Delaware

✓ AZUSA PACIFIC UNIVERSITY LIBRARIES
AZUSA, CALIFORNIA 91702-7000

© 1997 by Scholarly Resources Inc.
All rights reserved
First published 1997
Second printing 1998
Third printing 2001
Fourth printing 2003
Printed and bound in the United States of America

Scholarly Resources Inc.
104 Greenhill Avenue
Wilmington, DE 19805-1897
www.scholarly.com

Library of Congress Cataloging-in-Publication Data

Hart, Dianne Walta, 1939–
    Undocumented in L.A. : an immigrant's story / Dianne Walta Hart.
        p.   cm. — (Latin American silhouettes)
    ISBN 0-8420-2648-7 (alk. paper). — ISBN 0-8420-2649-5 (pbk. : alk. paper)
    1. Nicaraguan American women—California—Los Angeles—Interviews. 2. Nicaraguan American families—California—Los Angeles—Interviews. 3. Illegal aliens—California—Los Angeles—Interviews. 4. Immigrants—California—Los Angeles—Interviews. 5. Los Angeles (Calif.)—Biography. 6. Estelí (Nicaragua)—Biography. I. Title. II. Series.
F869.L89N53   1997
306.85'08968'7285079494—dc21   96-50993
                                                                        CIP

∞ The paper used in this publication meets the minimum requirements of the American National Standard for permanence of paper for printed library materials, Z39.48, 1984.

I dedicate this book

to my mother, Elizabeth Kranz Walta,

and to the memory of my father, Jack Walta.

Yamileth and I also would like to dedicate it to

Ken Bunker, who in August 1994, in his thirty-second year,

fell into God's hands from a ledge on Mount Adams

in the state of Washington

Acknowledgments

I would like to thank, always and especially, my husband, Tom, and our daughters Lisa, Heather, and Megan. I also would like to thank Olga Acuña, Rodolfo Acuña, Berta Aguilar, Marcus Borg, Linda Bricker, Keith Chambers, Loren Chavarría-Bechtel, Greg Connor, Rachelle Daniels, Sandy Enschede, Marian Ferring, Erin Logan Foley, Kayla García, Tim Getten, John Gilmore, Josette Griffiths, Barbara Hanrahan, Elsie Hart, Andrea Herling, Rigoberto Hernández Aguilar, George Keller, Judy Carlson Kelley, Dave and Jean Kliewer, Terrie Kolodziej, Gloria Levine, Sally Malueg, Brenda McCullough, Mike Morrissey, Mike Oriard, Cyd Perhats, Eric Piel, Kathy Poole, Sandra Rodríguez, Shirley Scott and the Oregon State University Valley Library for a research travel grant, Bob and Kitty Shepard, Stirling Smith, Griselda Solano, Angie Efthimiou Sutton, Ray Verzasconi, Doug Walta, Greg Walta, Alan Weiner, Bill Wilkins, Penny and Mark and their family, and all of Yamileth's family, both in the United States and in Nicaragua.

Contents

Foreword

*—This was the secret of America: A nation
of people with the fresh memory of old traditions
who dared to explore new frontiers.*
JOHN F. KENNEDY

—You are made to be in your own land.
YAMILETH (from South-Central Los Angeles)

—You have to work hard no matter where you are.
OMAR, YAMILETH'S BROTHER (from Nicaragua)

As we discover in this fascinating oral history, Yamileth is an undocumented Latina who has been struggling to survive in Los Angeles since January 1, 1989. We come to know her, however, over a period of more than ten years, following her, her son, and other family members from war-torn Nicaragua to strife-torn South-Central Los Angeles. Yamileth's story unfolds during a time when the number of documented and undocumented immigrants to the United States is approaching a historic high. In the 1980s some 8.7 million immigrants entered the United States, matching the number in the great immigration decade of 1901–1910. Given that the annual total has increased since 1991, the total for the 1990s could exceed 12 million people.

Relative to the size of the population, recent immigration is still well below the levels of the earlier part of this century. U.S. Census Bureau data indicate that in 1910 the foreign-born in the United States constituted about 15 percent of the total population, while, based on current immigrant levels, by the year 2000 the foreign-born may constitute 10 percent of the total population. Statistics, however, do not give us the complete picture of recent immigration. Who are these new immigrants?

The new immigrants began arriving in increasing numbers in the mid-1960s, for reasons not unlike those of their predecessors. The "push" factors included the foreign capital penetration of developing countries, dramatic population growth, the economic impoverishment of an increasing number of people, civil strife, and religious or ethnic persecution; the "pull" factors included increased job opportunities and, more important, significant changes in U.S. immigration law.

The 1965 amendments to the Immigration and Nationality Origins Quota System increased the total number of individuals permitted to enter the United States each year from 158,000 to 270,000, as well as the number of categories of persons who were exempt from these numerical limitations. They made it easier for legal residents to bring relatives to the United States and, influenced by the civil rights movement, also eliminated racially based barriers. These amendments reflected a conscious effort on the part of the U.S. government to encourage immigration in response to the demands of certain industries (for example, the garment industry, tourism, and agriculture) for a steady supply of cheap labor, a situation that mirrored the attempts by U.S. industrialists after the Civil War to import cheap labor from southern, central, and eastern Europe.

The 1986 amendments to the Immigration and Nationality Act, while reestablishing national origins quotas and attempting to halt the flow of illegal immigrants by enhancing border enforcement and imposing sanctions on employers who hired them, also granted legal status to an estimated 2.6 million illegal immigrants already in the country. The Immigration Act of 1990 further increased the levels of immigration, particularly employment-based immigration of highly skilled professionals, in response to the needs of America's high-tech industries, from semiconductors to biotechnology, which had become increasingly dependent upon foreign-born scientists, engineers, and entrepreneurs to remain globally competitive. Moreover, in response to the anti-Communist sentiments prevalent during the Cold War, other legislation has made it easier for political refugees to avoid quotas and enter the United States. The trend began with the Hungarians in 1955, and subsequently included Cubans, Vietnamese, Cambodians, Laotians, and Chinese, among others. As a result of these changes, by 1990 more than 1 million legal immigrants were entering the United States each year.

How are the new immigrants different from those of previous generations? From 1820 until 1870, a majority of immigrants came from the British Isles and northern Europe and, except for the Irish, were predominantly Protestant. After 1870 a majority came from southern, central, and eastern Europe. They were predominantly Roman Catholic and, for the first time, included a substantial number of Jews. Since the 1960s, however, political and economic stability in Western Europe has decreased the desire of people from that region to emigrate to the United States. As a result, only 12 percent of recent immigrants are from Europe, with the majority from central and eastern Europe. On the other hand, roughly 35 percent of recent immigrants are from Asia, 24 percent from Mexico, 13 percent from the Caribbean, and 11 percent from Central and South America.

Recent immigrants are also different from those of the early part of this century in that a high percentage (26.6 percent) holds university degrees. Education levels are highest for immigrants from India, the Philippines, China, and Korea, and lowest for those from Mexico and Central America. Recent women immigrants are only slightly less educated than men; 11.1 mean years of schooling for women versus 11.5 years for men reflect increased educational opportunities for women in developing countries. In addition, about 10.3 million foreign-born women were counted in the 1990 census, constituting 53 percent of the recent immigrants, and suggesting that, for the first time, not all women are "tied immigrants"—that is, not all women immigrate solely because of opportunities offered to male members of their families. While it has been suggested that the majority of the "non-tied" immigrant women are professionals (for example, 40 percent of the women doctors in the United States are foreign born), Yamileth and her sister may not be exceptions. Unfortunately, there is essentially no research on the subject.

Immigration to the United States has always been network driven, with the more recent immigrants often joining relatives, friends, or individuals from their own ethnic community. Just as Irish, Italian, Polish, Greek, and central and eastern European immigrants tended to settle in the metropolitan areas, particularly on the East Coast, the new immigrants have similarly congregated. Depending on which data we wish to consider (Census Bureau, Immigration and Naturalization Service, or various independent studies), California has absorbed 40 to 50 percent of the new immigrants, with Florida, New York, Illinois, Texas, New Jersey, and Arizona accounting for another 30 to 35 percent. Moreover, eight cities (Los Angeles, San Francisco, New York, Houston, San Antonio, Chicago, Miami, and Honolulu) have absorbed, and continue to absorb, the highest percentage. Furthermore, because of a drop in the fertility rates among the native-born, a higher fertility rate among recent immigrants, and a decline in return migration, since the 1960s immigration has accounted for an increasing proportion of the total population growth: from roughly 11 percent between 1960 and 1970, to 33 percent between 1970 and 1980, to 39 percent between 1980 and 1990. For the aforementioned cities and states, however, immigration now accounts, directly or indirectly, for more than 50 percent of the population growth.

The increase in undocumented immigrants also dates from the 1960s, abetted by the end of the Bracero Program (which for almost two decades brought thousands of rural Mexican males to work in U.S. agriculture during the harvest season every year). The fact that the demand for low-paid agricultural workers remained high created a pull effect, while Mexico's rapidly expanding population and, particularly after 1980, deteriorating economic situation created a push effect. A similar expanding population and social, political, and economic instability in most of Central America eventually created a tunnel effect. Emigration patterns in Central America have followed a familiar course: from countryside to city; from city to neighboring Costa Rica or El Salvador; to Mexico; and, finally, to the United States.

Various estimates put the total undocumented immigrant population in 1994 at between 3.2 and 3.8 million (with an estimated annual increase between 200,000 and 300,000). Of these, 1.2 to 1.7 million live in California, and another 1.1 to 1.7 million, in descending order, are distributed primarily in New York, Texas, Florida, Illinois, New Jersey, and Arizona. Again, depending on whose statistics we wish to believe, 50 to 80 percent of the undocumented immigrants in California live in the Los Angeles metropolitan area, and the vast majority are from Mexico and Central America. While some undocumented immigrants are individuals who remain in the United States after their student or tourist visas expire and are highly educated, the majority, like Yamileth and her family, probably have less than a high-school education and more than likely make the border crossing on foot.[1]

Despite whatever other differences may exist between recent and earlier immigrants, there is one striking similarity. Now, as then, the vast majority views the United States as a land of opportunity and, in the process, tends to exaggerate those opportunities when

---

[1]Precisely because they are undocumented, it is difficult for anyone to come up with reliable data on the numbers of these immigrants, their level of education, the proportion of men to women, or their country of origin. It also makes it extremely easy for anyone engaged in the political debate to manipulate the data to suit his own agenda.

contacting family or friends in their native land. Indeed, from the first day Europeans set their sights on the New World, they have engaged in such exaggeration. This was true of Columbus and most of the early Spanish chroniclers and remained true of the impoverished millions who arrived in the nineteenth and early twentieth centuries. As did Yamileth's sister, those who wrote home often played up their own success as a way of "saving face." And that vision, of an America whose streets are "paved with gold," was and is reinforced by the fact that many immigrants were and still are able to send money home, and also by the fact that the few immigrants who have managed to return home (permanently or to visit) have achieved a relative degree of economic success, at least in comparison to their compatriots. As we see in this oral history, in different ways both Yamileth and her sister, despite their poverty, contribute to the myth of an America whose streets indeed are paved with gold.

Recent anti-immigrant sentiment has made itself known in California's Proposition 187 which, if upheld by the courts, would deny, among other things, social services to legal and illegal immigrants, and schooling to the children of illegal immigrants. Such sentiment is also evident in the bill passed by the 104th Congress. While the final version signed into law by the president excluded the original House provision that would have turned the nation's teachers into immigration cops, the bill denies federal assistance to undocumented residents and access by legal immigrants (with certain exceptions) to Supplemental Security Income, Medicaid, Aid to Families with Dependent Children, food stamps, and certain child welfare benefits.

These anti-immigrant sentiments are not new. The first U.S. immigration laws date from 1882 and include the Chinese Exclusion Act, which was openly racist, and the first laws that placed restrictions on the admittance of "diseased persons, paupers, and other undesirables." By 1917, Congress had imposed a literacy test on all immigrants. The first quota law was passed in 1924 and provided for a national origins plan to be put into effect in 1929. The plan limited the annual number of European immigrants to 1/6th of 1 percent of the number of people of that origin in the United States in 1920, thus favoring immigrants from the British Isles and northern Europe. The 1924 Act also excluded all Asians.

Then, as now, antiforeign sentiments were reflected in increased crime and violence in metropolitan areas. Immigrants crowded into rat-infested housing and worked long hours for meager wages.

Surrounded by incredible wealth, not a few turned to crime, particularly organized crime. Alcohol and drugs (chiefly opium) not only helped to soothe the pain of many a newcomer but also led to an increase in related social problems. By the early part of this century, when Italians, Irish, and Poles began to organize to gain political clout, their political machines and labor union activities posed a new threat to the establishment, which moved quickly to attempt to undermine them. Then, as now, there was also considerable fear that the new immigrants were taking jobs away from native-born Protestant Americans and were depressing wages.[2]

Mostly, however, the southern, central, and eastern Europeans were different from the Anglo-Germanic peoples who constituted the dominant population. They prayed to a different God or gave their primary allegiance to the pope, ate strange foods, preferred wine over beer, and simply refused (or so it seemed) to adapt to "the American way." As a result, stereotypes flourished. These new immigrants were lazy, ignorant, and given to frequent fighting, drunkenness, crime, and other forms of uncivilized behavior. And then, as now, they were accused of refusing to learn English and of continuing to speak to their children in their native language.[3]

---

[2] One apparent difference, according to several 1996 polls, the results of which were reported in *Time, Newsweek,* and other national media, is that African Americans are still generally more supportive of immigration than Americans of European descent, even though a higher percentage is convinced that immigrants are denying them access to jobs and are depressing wages. In previous generations, the opinions of African Americans were not considered.

[3] On July 1, 1996, the U.S. House of Representatives passed H.R. 123, the English Language Empowerment Act, an emotionally charged but totally mangled version of numerous "English-only" bills that have failed in the past two decades. Despite overwhelming evidence that the vast majority of immigrants (documented and undocumented) is determined to learn English, the Republican leadership attempted to make "English only" a campaign issue. The irony, of course, escapes most people. In Los Angeles, English-language classes run twenty-four hours per day and usually carry a six-month, or longer, waiting list. At the same time, the Republican House leadership has proposed dramatic cuts in federal funding for English as a second language.

According to other 1996 polls, the results of which were also reported in the national media, as many as 80 percent of American citizens favor a constitutional amendment that would make English the official language of the United States, essentially asserting that most Americans expect new immigrants to accomplish in a few weeks or months what they themselves never accomplish in a lifetime—namely, gain a high degree of proficiency in a second language. Many of us who are children of immigrants and who spoke a heritage language at home

As in earlier decades, the current debate between the two presumed outcomes of the immigrant experience—assimilation and pluralism—is emotionally charged, with each side accusing the other of grossly distorting or manipulating data, particularly in terms of the economic costs and benefits of the new immigrants on the nation. The dominant sentiment of the assimilationists was probably best expressed by President Woodrow Wilson, addressing a group of newly naturalized citizens: "You cannot become thorough Americans if you think of yourselves in groups. America does not consist of groups. A man who thinks of himself as belonging to a particular national group in America has not yet become an American." Given the relative homogeneity of the early European immigrants and the fact that African Americans and American Indians were excluded from the national discourse, it is not surprising that assimilation long meant Anglo-Germanic conformity.

The pluralist idea of the United States as a melting pot was expressed by Michel-Guillaume Jean de Crèvecoeur in 1782 when he stated that people of all nations fused together to form a new race. Of course, until recently the pluralists viewed the melting pot as essentially European, if no longer exclusively Anglo-Germanic. Today, however, assimilation becomes problematic. Assimilation to what? And assimilation by whom? While a majority of Americans is most likely swayed by arguments relating to the costs and benefits of the new immigration (and the current discussion highlights the fact that costs and benefits are frequently determined by subjective criteria), underlying the debate are more fundamental issues. Can people from radically different cultures assimilate to the dominant Anglo-Germanic culture, or will the dominant culture be transformed? And if the dominant culture is transformed, will it be for the better or the worse?

In terms of costs and benefits, the new immigrants do have access to a host of public services that were not available to those who arrived earlier. Universal primary and secondary public education and most child labor laws date only from the 1930s, the same decade in which Social Security and other federal social welfare laws were enacted. The children of earlier generations of immigrants, as often as not, worked side by side with their parents in agriculture or factories and sweatshops. And many of the publicly

---

remember how ludicrous it was, a half-century or more ago, that, while we were required to study a foreign language in high school, we were not allowed to use any language other than English outside of the classroom.

funded social benefits that U.S. citizens now enjoy date only from
the 1960s. Therefore, aside from concerns about job security, rac-
ism, and the clash of cultures, which highlight much of the current
debate, there is also a great deal of resentment, often voiced as
"My grandparents" (or "My great-grandparents") "didn't get any
state or federal benefits, let alone a free public education. Why
should they?"

A fact that is undeniable is that seven states—California, New
York, Illinois, Florida, Texas, New Jersey, and Arizona—bear a
lion's share of the burden of providing the new immigrants and
their children social services and public education. Also undeniable is that many of the social services constitute unfunded or only
partially funded federal mandates, leaving residents of these seven
states with a disproportionate share of the costs of implementing
federal immigration and social service laws.

The new immigration has led to a wealth of scientific and liter-
ary works that deal with its causes and consequences, both for the
United States and the emigrant countries. Social scientists and his-
torians usually interpret "immigration" in purely physical terms and,
consequently, focus their attention on discovering specific causes,
such as economics, civil strife, religious or ethnic persecution, dramatic population increases, and changes in immigration policy.
These explanations, while certainly valid, do not help us to understand why one individual may choose to emigrate while his sib-
lings, even if offered the same possibility, may not. For example,
why Yamileth and her sister but not their brother?

Yamileth's attachment to Nicaragua remains the memory of her
dead mother, a maternal concern for her brother, and her devotion
to the revolutionary cause. But, as she switches from her dishes of
rice and beans to hamburgers, and as she decides to learn English,
one can only wonder if she, too, is not losing faith in that revolutionary cause; if she, too, as her sister seems to have already done,
has decided that there is no future in Nicaragua, however bleak her
prospects are in South-Central Los Angeles. One wonders if she
and her son will not, in an effort to overcome overt discrimination
and the disadvantages of being "outsiders," become more "American" than most Americans.

Human beings may have a dual nature—that is, a desire "to be
one with others," which leads us to anchor our roots in bedrock,
and a desire "to be other," which leads us to seek new frontiers of
the mind and soul, as well as of place. In some individuals and
perhaps even in some cultures, this drive "to be other" may be stron-

ger. In her own mind, Yamileth's decision to emigrate to the United States (a decision seemingly made without great forethought) may have seemed based solely on economic reasons. She would make money and return to Nicaragua where she would have a better life. As she says, "You are made to be in your own land." And she repeatedly insists that she is not a political refugee although, despite her determination to return to Nicaragua to work for the revolutionary cause, she expresses doubt about how safe she and her son would be.

Thus, through her own words and most likely without being aware of it, Yamileth also informs us that there may have been other forces at work in her decision to emigrate. Her peregrination, therefore, is not solely physical; it is psychological and spiritual and, as she perhaps ultimately realizes, cultural. To what extent does she feel oppressed by *¿el qué dirán?* (what will people say?) in terms of her sexual choices? To what extent does she feel oppressed by the ghost of her mother, whom she carries on her shoulders and who seems to have placed the care of the entire family in her hands? To what extent did the male leadership of the Sandinista Revolution, by seeking to empower women, doubly betray them when, following the triumph of the Revolution, it was unable to deliver on any of its promises?

Yamileth's testimony, which spans more than ten years, complements research in many disciplines. She exposes her fears, doubts, aspirations, and also her contradictions in ever-fluctuating moods. She helps to destroy stereotypes about immigrants (not just Nicaraguan or Latin American immigrants) and provides us with insights into the changing or static meaning of the word *familia*, the changing or static gender roles in developing countries, and the spiritual nature of those immigrants who, at some point, make a decision to leave their own countries.

Clearly, the political and economic situation in Nicaragua played a role in the decision of her sister and then Yamileth to emigrate to the United States, and that situation continues to influence Yamileth's decision not to return "just yet." The Sandinista Revolution, strongly supported by Yamileth and her family, triumphed in 1979, overthrowing the forty-six-year-long Somoza dictatorship. The Sandinistas, in an attempt to eliminate the worst of the social inequities, confiscated the Somoza lands and began to redistribute wealth and property. Many wealthy Nicaraguans left for Florida, but many of the people who remained were optimistic about the literacy campaign, free public education, and promises of free health care. And many women no doubt believed that they would play a significant role in the development of a new society.

In 1981, however, the Reagan administration suspended all U.S. aid to Nicaragua and eventually began to support the Contras (counterrevolutionary military groups). The low-intensity war conducted by the U.S.-backed Contras sapped the Nicaraguan budget and, after a time, brought to a halt the new social programs. A U.S.-imposed economic embargo also cut the country off from needed supplies. Disagreements and disputes broke out within the Catholic Church. The Sandinistas censored the press, thereby undermining their democratic claims. Refugees fled the agricultural areas in which the military conflicts raged, and floods and hurricanes ruined what was left of the crops. The military draft became increasingly unpopular. As the war forced the Sandinistas to spend up to 50 percent of the national budget on the military, inflation shot up, reaching as high as 14,000 percent annually. The situation was not helped by a bloated and inefficient bureaucracy that made buying a bag of cement impossible and rewarded military leaders rather than competent managers. By the late 1980s, when Yamileth and her family left, the dreams of most Nicaraguans were only fantasies of what might have been. For many, the dreams had become nightmares.

As a result, in 1990, Nicaraguans voted out Sandinista leader Daniel Ortega, electing Violeta Barrios de Chamorro president. Chamorro intended to reactivate the private sector (which the Sandinistas had ignored), but competing political forces compelled her to abandon many reforms. Juvenile delinquency and drug use increased dramatically, and unemployment surpassed 60 percent in some areas. A constitutional crisis soon pitted the executive branch against the legislature, and infighting became more important than problem solving. The pre-Sandinista sources of aid, such as the United States, seemed weary of the region and ready to wash their hands of Nicaraguan problems; and the Sandinista allies, such as Sweden and Spain, had little faith left in what might happen to their funds in Nicaragua. The bitter 1996 election, in which the mayor of Managua, Arnoldo Alemán, defeated the ever-present Daniel Ortega, set the stage for charges of corruption, and all sides fell to squabbling. No wonder Yamileth does not want to return just yet.

However, Yamileth's testimony is not a Nicaraguan story; it is a universal one that has been lived and suffered by millions of immigrants over the centuries and, no doubt, will be lived and suffered by millions more. We gain insights not only into the changing role of women in developing countries but also into the counterforces that work against such change, and into the point-counterpoint between devotion to family and the need for spiritual, as well as economic and sexual, liberation. Equally important, Yamileth provides us with insights into life (if it can be called that) in a strife-torn urban ghetto. This life, as Dianne Walta Hart notes when discussing the 1992 Los Angeles riots, has largely been ignored not only by the media but also by Latino political leaders.

Her testimony, therefore, helps us to better answer questions and concerns that are clearly on the minds of many Americans. Are the new immigrants bankrupting our social services? In what way are they different from those of past generations, if indeed they are? Will the new immigrants from Asia and Latin America import the very nature of the sociopolitical and economic institutions from which they flee, leading to the demise of American democracy? Or will they, like past generations of immigrants, eventually acculturate and, if so, what will be the acculturation model? Will they, as John F. Kennedy envisioned, help change institutions for the better? And, as Hart asks in her epilogue, what can the new immigrants teach us about ourselves and our own immigrant past?

Yamileth has found a good listener in Dianne Walta Hart. Her voice is never intrusive, yet she does not pretend to be the omniscient author who knows all there is to know about Yamileth. In the very best tradition of oral history, Hart reveals the questions that continually cross her mind and which arise from her realization that, given her own significantly different cultural background, Yamileth can never be fully accessible to her.

Undocumented in L.A. will contribute to the wide range of courses in immigration studies, urban studies, women's studies, and Latin American studies. More important, I believe, because Hart's sole concern is to provide us with in-depth insight into a recent immigrant and not to enter the debate on the pros and cons of current immigration policy, Yamileth's story allows readers to come to their own conclusions. Consequently, it is a most welcome addition to an increasing body of information on the subject.

Ray Verzasconi
Professor Emeritus of Spanish
Oregon State University

Introduction

I named her Marta a long time ago. It was a strong name that belonged to a strong person like Yamileth and had a crispness to it
that Yamileth had when she spoke. Certainly, someone named Marta
would have the same sharp humor she had, and Yamileth, as well
as I, liked the name. Nonetheless, I was often tempted to use her
real name because it caught more of her softness, her sadness, her
physical smallness, her uniqueness, her mischievousness, and her
fears. We initially decided to use pseudonyms to protect Yamileth
and her family. They, as many Nicaraguans, have often needed other
names, other identities, throughout much of their history. In
Yamileth's life, she needed pseudonyms to fight for the Nicaraguan
Revolution against Anastasio Somoza Debayle and his guardsmen,
then as she fought to protect the Revolution against U.S.-backed
Contras, and finally as she tried to find work in the United States
without legal documents.

Every time I interviewed Yamileth and the family, I asked if I
should continue using pseudonyms as I had in the first oral history
of the family.[1] In 1989, after Yamileth had been in the United States
for less than a month, she said, "I don't know about pseudonyms. I
don't know if I should be afraid to say how I came here. I really
have done nothing wrong. I'm not fleeing from anything. I'm not
here to say anything against anyone or anything. I won't know what
to think until I know what people say, what they think."

Eventually some of the family members thought that pseudonyms did not matter, even though several of them still had no legal papers. Yamileth, though, always the most cautious and the most
political one, had become even more cognizant of the reversals in a
country's political situation, the status of immigrants, and the deeply

---

[1]Dianne Walta Hart, *Thanks to God and the Revolution: The Oral History of
a Nicaraguan Family* (Madison: University of Wisconsin Press, 1990). The book
explores the family's history under the Somoza dictatorships (1933–1979), their
actively supportive roles in the struggle that preceded the 1979 triumph of the
Revolution, and their experiences under the governance of the Sandinistas (1979–
1990).

held opinions of some Nicaraguan political groups within the United States. She continued to insist on pseudonyms. As the manuscript neared completion, she agreed to use her real first name but wanted pseudonyms for everyone else, with the exception of Ken Bunker, who was Carlos in the first oral history of the family, and Mark and Penny, who befriended her.

When I first met Yamileth, I asked her the origin of her name since I had not heard it before. She said that her mother told her that she first heard the name on a radio program, and the family knew of other Yamileths in Nicaragua. Later, a scholar suggested that it came from the Hebrew, but the family knew only that their mother's tendency for giving imaginative names was passed on to all of them.

When Yamileth obtained her passport to leave Nicaragua, she found out she was five years older than she thought she was, placing her at that time in her late, rather than early, thirties. Later, I told her that at the rate she was getting older, we would soon be the same age. She laughed, leaned over to grab my arm, and said, "Well, that way we can talk with each other all our lives." And sometimes, it seems as if we have.

Every time I see her, I am again surprised by the smallness of her hands and features. She is less than five feet tall with frizzy brown hair that frames her light brown face and a ruddy complexion. She speaks quickly, her diction is crisp, and her eyes sparkle as if she were about to tell a ribald joke. Neighbors in Nicaragua affectionately call her *Negrita*, little black woman, and friends often shorten her name to Yami. She can be shy and reserved, but inevitably her humor and quick insight attract people. She has other intangible qualities that sustain her magnetism: directness, sincerity, and a mischievous sense of humor she inherited from her mother. She is proud, rarely cries, hates to depend on others, and insists on "paying her own way." Asking for favors, when she must, humiliates her; and when she speaks, she carries a sense of authority with her. At least she did in Nicaragua; in the United States, however, I have often heard her say, "*¿Qué sé yo?*" (What do I know?) In her hometown of Estelí, and especially in the Nicaraguan countryside where she feels most comfortable, Yamileth laughs easily and banters with people, showing her concern and intimate knowledge of their lives. Her strength belies her vulnerability. In unfamiliar situations, she becomes unsure of herself and of her social skills, shy to the point of barely speaking or eating. Living in Los Angeles has made her bashfulness more apparent.

I met Yamileth and her family in 1983 on a visit to Nicaragua.[2] The following year, when I was once again teaching Spanish at Oregon State University, I asked the family's permission to record their oral history. Although I knew Yamileth before the rest of her family, she was the one who seemed to trust me, and anyone else, the least quickly. She held back the longest, and watched me most carefully. Yet somehow she is the one I ended up knowing best. It took me a long time, though, to understand the one characteristic of Yamileth's that influences her the most: she is so afraid of losing those she loves that she cannot say no to them. It contradicts her strength of purpose and self, but that, I suppose, is the human condition.

Yamileth was born to María, a *campesina*, a peasant, in Nicaragua. Her father moved to Costa Rica before she was born, but her mother remembered him as the best of all the men she had known. The family was one of the poorest in town: the children—among them Yamileth, her older sister Leticia, and younger brother Omar— contributed to the household income by walking the streets selling *elotes* (ears of green corn) from trays on their heads, shining shoes in the park while they had no shoes of their own, and cleaning up after other people's children when they were children themselves. At the age of ten, Yamileth left a job in the tobacco fields to avoid having to become a supervisor's mistress. Occasionally a kind employer allowed her to attend school, and she eventually finished the sixth grade.

In the mid-1970s, Yamileth, Leticia, and Omar supported the Nicaraguan revolutionary struggle by working to overthrow the decades-long Somoza dictatorship. Omar joined the Sandinistas and spent two years fighting in the mountains, and Leticia provided a safe house in Managua for Omar and his fellow *guerrilleros*. Yamileth smuggled guns to the revolutionaries, spent a month in jail for refusing to tell the Somoza military where Omar was, and led her family—including her son born in 1976—out of Estelí as Somoza bombed it. She welcomed the triumph of the Revolution in July 1979 but grieved for her own losses: a brother killed in a

---

[2]I went to Nicaragua with the First Oregon Professional Women's Tour arranged by Margaret Thomas, then of the Eugene-based Committee in Solidarity with Central American People. We were accompanied by two women television reporters, Ann Curry (still with NBC) and Bebe Crouse (now a free-lance journalist in San Diego), and cameramen Kevin Feltz and Gary Kahne.

military ambush, a husband killed in the final battle, and the beginning of her brother Omar's lifelong depression.

After the 1979 triumph, Yamileth volunteered with the Asociación de Mujeres Nicaragüenses Luisa Amanda Espinoza (AMNLAE), the Sandinista Front-sponsored national women's organization, which eventually led to a paid position in the regional office. Although her formal education was limited, she discovered that through AMNLAE she could help other Nicaraguan women in the development of their country, which, in turn, gave meaning to her life. She used her artistic abilities to create banners that announced meetings and lectures; she taught women to drive tractors and to realize that they, too, had rights; she taught birth control and hygiene to campesinos. She worked in cooperatives, built maternity houses, and led delegations of inquisitive foreigners through the Nicaraguan countryside. In all, she helped build the community spirit that she and many Nicaraguans hoped would lead to a better country.

And then there was the house. For years the family had lived in a series of rented shacks and rooms, and some of their most wrenching and vivid childhood memories were of being chased out for not being able to pay the rent. In 1982, a block from one of the intersections of Estelí where the main banks were located, the Sandinista government appropriated land from Somoza followers and built some duplexes for low-income people. Yamileth was able to buy a duplex and moved in with her mother and young son. She fenced in their dirt-floored indoor-outdoor kitchen and planted trees and herbs in the tiny front yard. They were there to stay.

Estelí is renowned for its heroism. All through Nicaragua's history, it has played an important role. Some even call it "Estelí Heroico." Insurrections against Somoza's guards occurred in the city in September 1978 and again in April and July 1979. In 1978, Somoza ordered his air force to bomb Estelí for thirteen days, destroying more than one hundred businesses. In 1985 the Contras attacked nearby La Trinidad, a symbolic strike against Estelí, during which Yamileth stayed up day and night for well over a week, patrolling the outer edges of the city. The people there strongly supported the Sandinistas, and the few who supported the Contras, or who were indifferent, went quietly about their business. In the 1990 elections, Estelí was one of the few areas where the majority of the people voted for Daniel Ortega of the Frente Sandinista de Liberación Nacional (FSLN, or Sandinista National Liberation Front) rather than for Violeta Chamorro of the Unión Nacional

Opositora (UNO, or National Opposition Union). As the military conflict increased between the U.S.-sponsored Contras and the Sandinista army, Yamileth's work became paramilitary, and she taught women in cooperatives how to defend themselves from Contra attacks. Much of her work took place in the most hazardous areas of Nicaragua, and her life was often in danger from a Contra ambush on the road, an attack on a cooperative, or just being in the wrong place at the wrong time.

When Yamileth left AMNLAE in 1987 to take care of her dying mother, she continued helping the women's organization whenever she could. Her work, either as an employee or as a volunteer, brought with it the satisfaction of helping the *campesinos* she so dearly loved, the pride of harvesting corn and beans, the fulfillment of aiding Nicaragua the way she knew best, and the joy of being with people who loved her. In the meantime, war and bureaucracy relentlessly sapped Nicaragua's budget and the people's revolutionary spirit. Desperate decisions were made. In 1988, a few months after their mother, Doña María, died, Yamileth's sister Leticia left Nicaragua to join her husband, Sergio, in the United States. Hoping to make enough money to support the family from afar, Leticia left her four daughters behind in Yamileth's care. Leticia and Sergio intended to return to Nicaragua with their savings, but eight months later, Leticia decided that the girls should join them in Los Angeles. Yamileth and her son agreed to accompany them on their trip to the United States, where perhaps she could realize her dream of buying a VCR.

Yamileth said, "I called right back and said yes." That call from Estelí to Leticia in Los Angeles in the fall of 1988 symbolized the beginning of her life in the United States and of the recognition of the end of her personal dream for the success of the Nicaraguan Revolution; nonetheless, had anyone had the foresight at that moment to point that out to her, she would have fiercely denied any such significance. As with most decisions, hers was made in small steps that led, little by little, to lifetime changes.

Her decision was not unlike that of many others who, for one reason or another, have chosen to leave their native land. Yamileth describes herself as an economic refugee, and she steadfastly refuses to give up her Nicaraguan citizenship. Going home, however, proves to be more impossible each day, yet staying in the United States continues to be difficult. Only through knowing the López family have I learned to profoundly understand the word "dilemma": no choice is the right choice. The small decisions that start with the small step end up being big decisions. And the decisions become lives, not for just one person but for whole families.

Neither Leticia nor Yamileth asked me what I thought about their coming to the United States, and I do not know what I would have replied had I been asked. Their move, however, provided a continuation of my study of their lives, which happened quite naturally when I invited Yamileth to our home after her arrival. There, as I had done every other time when we got together, I brought out the tape recorder. Thus, the story went on.

It is called methodology, but that seems to be too formal a word to explain why two women are sitting and talking at a kitchen table for a whole day or in a living room late in the evening. As I look back over a decade and a half, it all seems like a blur. We stay the same on the inside, but our faces get older, our hair grows or is cut, and mine grays while hers is now colored red. Our clothes change, and so do the questions and the locations. But we keep on talking, like some odd couple, looking like computer images that allow us to age while we shift in our chairs.

We speak in Spanish; later, I have the tape-recorded conversations transcribed, and then I translate them into English. When I first interviewed the family in 1984, I went to Nicaragua with carefully worded questions broken down into categories. I also had a so-called general page, waiting for the time when I had nothing to ask and they appeared to have nothing to say. Gradually, I became comfortable with silences, especially as I learned the hard way that silence often brought out more in the speaker, certainly more than did my interfering leaps into their thoughts. With the help of oral historian Mike Morrissey, I developed techniques and expressions that allowed me to broach subjects that I thought might be sensitive. My questions always focused on their personal lives, and the political aspects were told through their own experiences. Every year I reviewed the transcripts of the previous interviews, looking for anything incomplete, confusing, or contradictory, from which I fashioned a new set of questions, or, in later years, simply short notes to myself.

As the family and I relaxed and got to know each other better, the method evolved to my asking them about people or situations, and then letting them take the lead. I would interrupt only to clarify words or indefinite antecedents, but other than that, I let them talk. When I did that correctly, or when the mood was right, or when the discussion lent itself to that method, I had my best interview. When, for whatever reason, I had to interrupt a lot, the interview obviously did not flow as well. I often interjected questions that allowed me to get a better visual picture of the scene or of how they felt.

My intention has been to provide the reader with a smooth-flowing oral history that is entirely true to Yamileth's life. To do that, I have had to make decisions about what testimony to include in the manuscript; and, in general, I have selected a narrative that moves the story along. When my questions led Yamileth into areas of more self-exploration or in a direction that she would not naturally go, I made it apparent in her responses or occasionally included the questions in a rhetorical fashion in the text. When I was unsure of what she meant, I omitted the information rather than quote Yamileth incorrectly.

Midway through the interviews that I conducted after the completion of the first manuscript, I decided to work primarily with Yamileth. In Nicaragua, I had interviewed four members of the family; they rotated shifts, so to speak, in such a way that I always had someone to interview. But Doña María had died and Omar was still in Nicaragua, and although Leticia was in Los Angeles, she was so committed to her beauty salon that it was difficult to find time to talk; she ran the salon the same way she had in Nicaragua, which meant that clients rarely made appointments. As a result, she had to be there in case anyone showed up; fortunately for her, work was better in Pico-Union than it had been in Estelí. In addition, when our November 1989 interview lasted only three hours, shortened by the presence of a new boyfriend, I knew that her interest in the history had diminished. Although Leticia is not the protagonist of this story, her influence can be seen in nearly every event. When I visited the family in Los Angeles, I either interviewed or saw Leticia, but I spent considerably more time with Yamileth.[3]

Within her testimony (set off by large opening and closing quotation marks), I have interrupted in order to clarify or to set up what is to follow. The reader will also hear Yamileth address me, as is normal in any conversation. The final chapters are devoted to an

---

[3]Yamileth came to see Tom, me, and our children in Oregon in 1989, and she later visited in 1995 and 1996. I visited her in Los Angeles in 1989, again in 1990, twice in 1992, once in 1994, and every year after that. Yamileth and I often talk on the telephone, especially during times of crisis or change. Lisa and Megan (two of our daughters) have also visited her, and occasionally friends who are traveling through Central America stop to visit Omar in Estelí. I have not been back to Nicaragua since 1987.

analysis of her life within cultural and historical contexts and to the times when our lives bumped uneasily and joyfully into each other's. However, this will be her story, and mine only when our paths cross. It starts in Nicaragua.

People in Yamileth's Life

Yamileth López was born around 1955 in Estelí, Nicaragua. (Some birth dates are given; all are approximations.) Her mother, **Doña María López**, was born in 1919 and died in 1987. Her sister **Leticia** was born in 1947, and her brother **Omar** in 1956. Other people who have played a role in Yamileth's life story are:

Alan, a California teacher
Alejandra, her longtime friend and coworker in AMNLAE
David, her lover
Eddie, a Latino and a citizen of the United States
Gustavo, a Sandinista
Irene, Omar's wife, b. 1961
Ken Bunker, an American schoolteacher who lived with the
    López family in Nicaragua while studying Spanish
Lupe, Sergio's sister in Los Angeles
Manuel, a Mexican married to Marisa, b. 1968
Miguel, her son, b. 1976
Mundo, Sergio's brother, the *coyote*
Nilda, her sister in Managua, b. 1949
Penny and **Mark**, her Oregon employers
Roberto, Leticia's Salvadoran boyfriend
Rocío, Sergio's sister in Mexico City
Sergio, Leticia's husband, b. 1949
    Marisa, Leticia and Sergio's daughter, b. 1971
    Sofía, Leticia and Sergio's daughter, b. 1973
    Chela, Leticia and Sergio's daughter, b. 1975
    Nora, Leticia and Sergio's daughter, b. 1981
Tomás, my husband, Tom
Yolanda, her longtime friend and coworker in AMNLAE

One

The Death of the Morning Glory

*—You're like the morning glory that opens happily at dawn
and closes up tightly at night.*

Yamileth's mother had been sick for a long time, probably with congestive heart failure, and Yamileth went to talk with the doctor every day. I had last seen Doña María in August 1987; and when I left Nicaragua, I knew I would probably never see her again. By September, her feet were so swollen that she had not been out of bed for weeks. The doctor put her on vitamins and told Yamileth that there really was nothing to be done. By then, even Doña María was telling Yamileth not to give her any more medicine. She was dying, she said, and Yamileth's efforts were in vain. She begged not to be taken to the hospital where they would torment her with injections.

She improved enough by November to sit outdoors, in front of her side of the small duplex, and watch the people go by as she so loved to do. A neighbor said, "Oh, Doña María, today you woke up happy. You're finally smiling. You're like the morning glory that opens up happily at dawn and closes up tightly at night."

Doña María answered, "I don't know why sick people always get worse as night comes."

"That's when you feel death much closer," the neighbor replied.

Yamileth wanted her mother to have some tests at a lab two blocks from their duplex. The walk took them forty-five minutes, moving slowly, sitting down, getting up, walking some more, sitting again, and finally laughing because they knew that people must think they were crazy. The lab results showed a kidney infection, complicated by her weak heart and retained water. There was nothing to do, so Yamileth gave her herbal remedies, mainly roots, to refresh her stomach, liver, and kidneys. Death was close.

"On December 20, 1987, my mother's sister came to visit her in Estelí. My son Miguel and I were playing jacks when I overheard my mother tell her that what worried her is that Miguel and I, of all her family, would suffer most when she died. We had lived with her longer than anyone else, and she loved Miguel as if he were her own son. Then she told my aunt that there were still lots of things she needed to tell us. I pretended I didn't hear her, but I felt something in my heart telling me that she was going to die soon.

"Around eight o'clock in the evening, a car came by to announce the death of Ramón, a friend of hers.[1] For years, they had loved each other like brother and sister. Long ago, when she washed clothes in the river, he used to come by to talk with her. He even had the same disease as she. As soon as she heard the announcement of his death, she yelled, 'Oh, no! Who died? Ramón died? And now those poor daughters, what will they do? That poor woman, what will she do?' The doctor had warned us against giving her bad news, so I gave her a pill and we changed the subject, but it was useless.

"So that I could take care of her, I slept with her. The next morning she got up at half past four to go to the bathroom. After she came back, I saw her sitting on her bed. When you take care of a sick person, there are times when you're overcome with fatigue, and that's what happened to me. I fell asleep. An hour later, I woke up quickly, scared. She was still seated but bent over and snoring.

" 'Mama, mama,' I cried. 'Lie down. Lie down. I'll make you comfortable and fix your pillow. The doctor said you can't sleep sitting up.' She didn't answer me. I tried to lay her down, but she fell limply into bed. Miguel went crazy and ran down the street yelling for people to help. A neighbor helped me dress her so we could take her to the hospital. My mother had earlier told me not to hospitalize her, but I wanted to save her life. I didn't want her to die.

"I ran to the hospital, but the ambulance was out helping other people. I ran to the Red Cross, but the ambulance had just left for somewhere else. Then I found an uncle who had a military-type vehicle, and he went with me to get her. At the hospital, the doctor said that Ramón's death had affected her and that before Ramón

---

[1]In Nicaraguan towns the bereaved family would hire a car that had a public address system mounted on its roof. The driver would then cruise through the streets and broadcast the news of the death.

died, he, too, had been affected the same way by the death of someone else.

"They worked on her, but all I could think about was that I had
promised I wouldn't take her to the hospital; she wanted to stay at
home. As a result, I didn't even want to be there with her. The doctor told me there was no hope, she was going to die. I really didn't
want to see her suffer. I didn't want to always have the image of
her in a hospital in my mind. I'd rather think of her as alive, talking
with me, sharing moments of happiness and sadness and, as always, telling me jokes.

" 'Go,' Leticia said, 'and do what needs to be done.' I ran down
the street as if my mother's life depended on my speed and agility.
I felt that if I ran faster, she wouldn't die. In preparation for her
death, Omar borrowed a vehicle from the military to pick up my
mother's body from the hospital. All the neighbors came to help
me get the house ready. Don Ramón's family brought coffee, some
flowers, and sugar. A neighbor who works with Omar brought rice,
beans, and cigarettes. Omar's friends at work took care of the grave
site.

"All that was left to buy was the coffin, but I didn't even have
five cents. Then I remembered that she had been making payments
to a funeral home to pay for her coffin, so I went there. With all the
inflation in Nicaragua and the *córdoba* changing value all the time,
she had gotten behind in her payments. The woman in charge said
that she wasn't in the habit of giving out coffins if the full payment
hadn't been made. So I went to my niece Marisa, Leticia's daughter, and she gave me some money. I went back to the woman and
asked, 'Could you take this in the meantime? Later I'll pay the rest,
but I need the coffin now.' She agreed to do so.

"The problem was that I didn't need the coffin right then. I'd
need it later, after my mother died, to bring her home from the
hospital, so I told the woman I'd come back when that happened.
She said, 'If you come after eight o'clock tonight, I won't be able
to help you,' as if there were a time to die, a schedule or something! So around half past seven—just in time but still before my
mother died—Omar picked up the coffin, along with a statue of
Christ and some candles. When we got to the barrio with the coffin, people thought my mother had already died and we had her in
the coffin. So we had to explain that the doctors said my mother
would die within an hour and that the woman who sold us the coffin had put us in this awkward spot.

"The doctor transferred her to the hospital a few miles south in La Trinidad and put her on oxygen, keeping her alive artificially. She died that night between half past eight and nine o'clock. Leticia and Omar were with her. I was the only one not there. We never found out what she wanted to tell us, and I can't imagine what it might have been.

"The woman in the funeral home made a shroud for my mother. It was pink with long sleeves and white lace and had little roses around the collar and wrists. I didn't ever see the shroud on her, though. I never saw her after I left the hospital. I didn't want to. I didn't even look in the little window in the coffin.

"She came home in the coffin around nine-thirty that night. Neighbors made coffee, and one offered us his truck to take the coffin to the church and later to the cemetery. We decorated the truck and coffin with flowers. People brought red roses and yellow and purple chrysanthemums, and so did the neighborhood children whom she had always let come in the house to watch television. AMNLAE and the Mothers of the Heroes and Martyrs[2] each sent a beautiful bouquet. My friends at work took up a collection to make a cement cross so that we wouldn't lose my mother in the cemetery.

"Our custom is to have a prayer that lasts for nine days. The day after her death, we had a Mass and on the ninth day we went to the cemetery. The Mass was at six in the evening, and later people came to the house to drink coffee, eat bread, and smoke cigarettes. If you have a photo of the dead person, you put it near the coffin, on the wall. So we hung a photo that you had taken and left it there for the nine days of prayer.

"Some people stayed for only a short time, some longer, coming and going until six o'clock the next morning. Our house is so small that most people were outside. People stood around and talked, sometimes about her life, how she looked when she was sick, that it didn't seem that she was dead, what will these poor people do now that they were alone, things like that. Others laughed, who knows about what.

"After she died, I didn't want to see my brothers and sisters. I wanted to be alone, my son and me. She used to tell me, 'Don't be afraid, my dear daughter. If I die, I'll be with you at night. I'll

---

[2]The organization of Mothers of the Heroes and Martyrs helps the mothers and families of those who fought and died in Nicaragua's wars. The membership consists of the mothers, and Doña María had been an active participant.

come to you. Don't ever hit Miguel and make sure that no one yells at him. I'll take care of you wherever I am.' My poor dear mother.**"**

Leticia called to tell me the sad news on December 21, two hours after Doña María died. Even though Sergio had left months earlier for the United States, she had stayed in Nicaragua, partly out of obligation to her mother. With his departure, many of the financial responsibilities for the entire family had fallen on her shoulders, but there was no way to support everyone. In a sense, her mother's death freed her, and she immediately began looking for ways to leave Nicaragua.

But for Yamileth, who stayed behind, it was different. She said, "When people see that I don't have a mother, they'll start to talk about me. They'll look for a way to destroy me because they'll think I've turned to the streets to survive."

Yamileth did not have to turn to the streets, as her neighbors had speculated, but she did continue her secret affair with her lover, David. Her romance with him had developed against the backdrop of the war with the Contras. After their years of working and fighting for the Sandinista cause, Yamileth and David united politically and romantically, finding clandestine moments for each other in the midst of the military struggle. The intrigue and danger of war made the hours stolen for talking and for lovemaking all the more precious and exciting.

Starting in early 1986, Yamileth's friends arranged for her to see David at least once a month. After Yamileth quit work in 1987 to take care of her mother, her friend Alejandra would come from the AMNLAE office and, in front of the family, tell her about a problem at work—somewhere outside the city of Estelí—that only Yamileth could solve. The problem was always real, but it also allowed her to meet David, usually in the north, close to the hazardous Honduran border. When Yamileth still had her job with AMNLAE, she would be in the north for two or three months at a time. When David was stationed closer to Estelí, they would meet at a friend's house. No matter where they were, however, they had to be discreet. Yamileth's reputation as a woman and as a grassroots organizer was at stake; David, as a soldier, also had to watch his conduct. Such behavior was not considered proper for either one.

Yamileth and David had an agreement. "I told him: 'The day that you tire of me, or I tire of you, or we both tire of being in this situation, then we'll finish this peacefully without any problem.

We'll be friends.' He agreed and added, 'The day that you find another man, I'll give you the time you need. No problem.' He told me that, and so it is. No problem. Really, I can't be with him all the time, perhaps not in the moments he most needs me, or when I need him."[3]

None of her family knew then of her relationship with David, nor do they today. She told only her good friends from AMNLAE and me. She and I gave him a pseudonym, and I have never asked for his real name, although I have seen it on a document. I have never met him, either. Doña María and Miguel have but, according to Yamileth, they never suspected that she and David were lovers.

"David has another woman, and they have two children. That's a problem, and I'm in the middle. He used to justify our relationship because he and she were separated, but then he returned to her, and now they're together, not married, but together. They have a normal life. Well, maybe not completely normal because he has been stationed far from their home, and now he's in Estelí, my hometown.

"Out of respect for my mother and son, I didn't bring him to the house, but after my mother died, he often came to see me. We took Miguel out to eat, or they watched television together and talked. All I know was that I liked being with him.

"Miguel doesn't know I love David, probably because I don't view what David and I have between us as something that will establish itself permanently in my house, like a man who lives there, a father to my son. It's not right to tell Miguel that this man is coming to live with me. It's just not right. David has a woman he lives with, his own children, his own home.

"I found out he had two children before I quit work to take care of my mother. Right away, I called him on the phone at work—avoiding his house out of respect for the woman he lives with and their children—and told him he had to come to see me because I couldn't go there. I didn't tell him why.

"He came to the house where I was staying, near the border in Jalapa. He admitted he had gone back to her and they had two children, but he hoped that wouldn't change things between us. At that moment, I felt terrible, embarrassed, and even afraid that she'd find out I was there. I'm scared of such things because there are repercussions for a woman. It wasn't right that I, as a representative of a

---

[3]Hart, *Thanks to God and the Revolution*, 188.

mass organization of women, was in that situation. I avoided going north again.

"Later, when he was transferred to Estelí, I wasn't working, so things changed. But I still worry that someone will say that he came to my house, little things like that. I wouldn't continue this if I were a problem in his home. If I thought she was aware of me and she wanted to talk, I hope we'd do so as adults. David doesn't want to leave either one of us.

"So the solution depends on me. I'm the one who's a little at fault. He's with her because he loves her and the children. Since she has his children, she's not going to tolerate much. So someone has to make the decision. That's the way it is. You win some and lose some."

On April 21, 1988, Leticia called me from Brownsville, Texas, to tell me that she was on her way to join Sergio in Miami, where he had found work in a bicycle factory. Once in Miami, Leticia worked for several months by filling in at beauty salons. Eventually an old friend from Nicaragua offered her a position in a Los Angeles salon. Since Leticia was feeling uncomfortable in Miami's anti-Sandinista atmosphere,[4] she and Sergio packed their few belongings in their secondhand car and headed west.

Their daughters—Marisa, seventeen; Sofía, sixteen; Chela, fourteen; and Nora, seven—were still living in Estelí with Yamileth and Miguel in the duplex. It had two dark bedrooms, a combination living and dining room, and one bathroom. Wooden slats instead of glass covered the one window area, so the only light came in from the open front door. The living-dining room was furnished with a wooden table, one wooden chair, three plastic chairs, a dresser, a television set, and sometimes (depending on the economy) a refrigerator. They had running water and a door that locked. Every morning, they would clean the floor by sprinkling sawdust on it and sweeping it out. Behind the house was the *solar*, an indoor-outdoor kitchen with two wood-burning stoves on a dirt floor. Adjacent to the *solar* was a garden, chicken coop, and clothesline, all walled in by uneven boards placed at some distance from each other.

---

[4]Many of the Nicaraguans who were unhappy with the Revolution fled in the years after 1979. The country lost close to one thousand professionals per year, and many of them relocated in Miami, as had the Cubans before them. Since Contra political announcements came from Miami, the political ambience there was not one in which most Sandinista supporters felt comfortable.

The boards did not keep out the wind and rain; they served only to
mark off the area. It was clearly their property, which always made
Yamileth proud.[5]

"We all got along well in Estelí. Certainly, there were moments
when Marisa, or mainly Chela, tried to humiliate me by saying,
'Tía [Aunt] Yamileth, the only reason you have food is because my
mother sends money.' But, really, I didn't owe them anything.
Leticia had asked me to move to her house to take care of her children, but I told her I wouldn't and instead they could come to my
house. If I'd gone to hers, eventually the girls would have kicked
me out. If I'd told them not to go to parties, not to go to the movies,
they'd have done exactly what they wanted to do. At least in my
house, they had to obey what I said.

"The only thing I really couldn't tolerate was the mess they
made: clothes thrown everywhere and dirty clothes mixed with clean
clothes to the point that you didn't know which was which. They
had friends over, days, evenings, weekends, and I told the girls it
was embarrassing that their friends see such disorder. The house
was small, and the clothes should have been folded, at least. So
many friends came that I'd close myself in a bedroom.

"At the beginning, Leticia said that the money she sent to Nicaragua was mine since I was the one responsible for the girls, but
when she actually sent the money, she addressed it to Marisa, her
oldest daughter. The reality was the opposite of what Leticia had
said because instead of my being the one who was taking care of
the girls, Marisa was taking care of me. I still had the responsibility for my house, but not for the food we needed or how the money
would be spent. It was difficult for me and for Miguel because neither of us was used to begging. All that time, he never had money
to buy an apple or a banana, but the older girls did.

"There is food in Nicaragua, but only if you have money. The
problem is that the majority of people have no work and no money.
Both Marisa and her sister Sofía could have made money as hair-
dressers, but they'd gotten used to waiting for the money Leticia
sent. When they wanted to work, they did. When they didn't, they
didn't."

---

[5]Hart, *Thanks to God and the Revolution*, 9.

Two

Adios, Nicaragua

—You are made to be in your own land.

Leticia's decision to leave Nicaragua and then to move to Los Angeles set the stage for the rest of the family. In November 1988 she called Yamileth to tell her to get her daughters ready because she wanted them to come to the United States. The girls already had passports, and Yamileth obtained visas for them.

Leticia called back and asked, "Do you and Miguel want to come, too?" The reasoning, according to Yamileth, was that she would keep the girls company on the trip and then find work in the United States. The extra money would benefit all of them, and Yamileth could return afterward to Nicaragua with money to live on and to use to improve her house. Yamileth asked about job possibilities; Leticia said that there might be work taking care of children or elderly women, and Yamileth knew from experience that she would like that. The trip would be an adventure, she thought.

Although Yamileth no longer worked formally for the Sandinistas, she did volunteer work for them and knew her loyalty would be questioned if she left for the land of the enemy. Leticia pressed her for a decision. The *coyote* (a smuggler who brings illegal immigrants across the border) was Uncle Mundo, Sergio's brother, and he needed to know how many people would be going. In addition, he wanted to take advantage of the upcoming holidays— a traditionally slow time for border crossings—hoping that fewer patrolmen would be on the job. Still, Yamileth asked for a little time.

"I talked with Miguel, who said he wanted to go because he believed, from what Leticia and other people had told him, that it'd be like going to another world, to a paradise where everything would

be within our reach. He had always told me that if I got better work
or if we went to the United States, he'd like a bicycle, and I've
always wanted a VCR.

"I called Leticia right back and said yes. Then I went to my
friends Alejandra and Yolanda. 'Guess what?' I quietly and secretly
confided in them. 'Leticia's giving me the opportunity to go to the
States to make money quickly. Then I'd come back here to work,
and I'd fix up the house.'

"Alejandra, who had a sister in the States, said, 'Maybe everything will go well for you, like for my sister.[1] But not all people
have the same luck.'

"Yolanda said, 'Try it and see what happens. If it goes well for
you, all the better. If not, you can always come back here.'

" 'But what if I can't come back?' I asked.

" 'Then find something to do there, anything. Be yourself. Just
be the joker you usually are until they get to know you, and then
they'll learn to like you,' said Alejandra.

"They wanted to have a farewell party, but I told them not to do
that because a farewell party is when you're never going to come
back. What bothered me most, though, was that I wouldn't be there
for the upcoming anniversary of my mother's death.

"Alejandra said, 'Don't worry. I'll pay for the Mass and find
the person to pray at the house. We'll do everything as if you were
here. Don't worry. Go, go.'

"Still, I was afraid. I talked to a neighbor who reassured me,
'Don't be a fool. Try it. You'll lose nothing by trying.'

"My fear was that I might not be able to return because I'd be
so far away. I also worried about crossing the border. People told
me you had to walk I-don't-know-how-many kilometers. Others
said you had to cross a river, and many had drowned. Sometime
earlier, five people going to the States from Estelí were crossing a
river—I don't know what river—that had risen, and they all
drowned.

"I thought, 'I've got to get out of here. I don't have a job and
have no money. But what if I go someplace and die? Or if I'm not
the one who dies, but one of the girls is? No, if one of us is going to
die, better that we all die.'

"I didn't sleep much. I talked with my brother Omar. He said,
'I'm not telling you to go or stay. You're responsible for your own

---

[1]The sister was eventually caught by the Immigration and Naturalization
Service (INS) and spent time in a Miami jail.

actions and you know what you want, if you want to go or not. Personally, I wouldn't like to go because people tell me it's a lie that you can have anything you want. Anywhere in the world, you have to work hard to have something. If I wanted to have more, I'd have to work harder than I do now. It's true I don't live well, but we're more or less all right. If I get sick here, I get paid. If you get sick there, they aren't going to pay you.' Then he asked, 'What are you going to do with the house?'

" 'Well, that's what I wanted to ask you. Can you take care of it, live in it for three or four months, until I come back?'

"He agreed but added, 'It's going to be difficult in the United States. I don't believe you'll be back that soon.'

" 'Oh, yes, I will,' I said. 'As soon as I get there, I'll get a job, and the second month I'll send you some money.'

" 'Okay. When you're ready to leave, I'll go along with you to wherever you have to go.'

"Just before I was to leave, David came to Estelí to see me. By then, he knew I was going to the United States. He thinks a lot like Omar, so he asked, 'What are you going to do there?' I had told him about your family—Diana, Tomás, and all the daughters—so I said I was going to see you. I added, 'Leticia visited them once and gave talks about the Revolution.[2] The family helped her and they want me to go there.'[3] 'Look,' he said, 'I really don't want you to leave. It'd be better if you made a tape recording with all Diana wants to know and sent it along with someone else who's going there.'

"The situation in Nicaragua was difficult, so when people left, they needed to say that they were going to speak for the Revolution or, when they returned, be able to show some proof that they had. If you didn't do that, people thought you were running away from it. So I told him I was going to talk about the Revolution. I didn't tell him I intended to work to help Leticia pay back some money,[4] and also to finance some of my projects in Nicaragua, like improving my house.

"He was upset, so I went with him to a party outside of Estelí. We each had three beers and a good time, and the next day he took

---

[2]In 1986, Leticia spoke to Spanish classes at Crescent Valley High School and at Oregon State University, both in Corvallis.

[3]The fact is that Yamileth had not told me about her plan; Leticia later informed me of it.

[4]Yamileth has still not been able to pay Leticia.

me back. That was December 12, 1988. I told him I might leave that week, but he said he lived too far away, in Jalapa, to return to say goodbye. I said I'd come back soon. I can't write him now or call him because he's a soldier and not allowed to communicate with anyone living in the United States. What I can do, though, is talk to Alejandra and find out about him that way.

"The days went by. Leticia sent part of the money. It wasn't enough for all of us—the four girls, Miguel, and me—but she promised more would be coming soon and wanted us to get ready. Soon, Marisa and I decided to send three of the children ahead, on what we call an excursion, to Guatemala. Nicaraguans go there on a shopping tour to buy products you can't get in our country. Marisa couldn't go with them because the rest of the money was being sent to Managua under her name and she had to pick it up. The woman who ran the shopping excursion was a good friend of Leticia's, so I asked her to take Sofía, Chela, and Miguel to another one of Leticia's friends in Guatemala City. Marisa, Nora, the youngest, and I waited for the money, knowing that the next tour was leaving on the fifteenth.

"The only people the government of Nicaragua denied visas to were soldiers because they've promised to work, a promise they need to fulfill until they're released. After that, soldiers can travel with no responsibility to the government. Because I was so closely tied to the Sandinistas and the military, I was reluctant to tell many people about the trip. Just a few people knew I was leaving. Also, if a lot of people know you're going to the States, they say, 'Bring me this and bring me that.' The girls' friends would have said, 'Bring me shoes, dresses.' Still, I'm not afraid to show up in Nicaragua tomorrow with nothing. I didn't say I was coming back with a brand-new car. I just said I'd try living in the States, that it'd be an adventure. I told my friends we'd say goodbye to each other as if I were going to another city, one close to Estelí. I even told Alejandra and Yolanda, 'Don't get excited about it. I might be killed on the road.' They said, 'Don't be crazy! Of course you'll get there.'

"My friends asked me to write, not to forget them. I don't know why, but when people go to the States, they don't write to their friends anymore. I warned them it wasn't my custom to write to anyone. I like to write, but I start a letter and then get involved in something else. It's easier to talk. I can order my thoughts while I talk, but when I write, it all gets confused.

"So a couple of days later Marisa went to Managua to pick up the fifty dollars Leticia had sent, and we left the 17th or 18th of

December. Omar and his wife Irene accompanied us to a bus stop at half past two in the morning. The tour bus leaves at that hour so that it can reach the Honduran border early and have less of a delay there.

"We waited and waited, but I finally realized the bus wasn't going to come. About ten yards away, I saw a man starting his van, which had Guatemalan license plates. I asked if he could take the three of us—Marisa, Nora, and me—with him. He said he could take us through El Salvador to Guatemala, and we left soon afterward. But it turned out that he was going in another direction, to Espino and then to El Salvador, so we asked him to drop us off at the Somoto intersection [in Nicaragua], which he did around half past six in the morning. Since we had Honduran visas, it was better to go that way instead of through El Salvador.

"We waited there more than fifteen hours. Finally, a tour bus on an excursion came by, and Marisa motioned for it to stop. The driver asked if we had reservations. Marisa said we didn't, but if there was space available, we'd like to go to Guatemala. We said we'd pay. The driver asked if we had passports, so we showed them to her. She agreed to take us, but since we were now part of her tour, she kept our passports until we got to Guatemala.

"We spent a long time at the Honduran border. We talked with no one in the bus because it had come from Managua, and we didn't know anyone. We don't trust strangers. We don't know who they are, and they don't talk to us, either. People from Managua are different from the people who come from the north. They don't communicate well, so it's not always that we're scared to talk, but that sometimes they just don't give us the opportunity.

"We traveled all day through Honduras. All Nicaraguans lack culture, but it seems to me that Hondurans lack a little bit more. There are more illiterates there. And they're rude. Maybe that's their style, I don't know. The place seems sad. No country is nice when you have to stay there a long time, only your own country. You are made to be in your own land.

"Since we got to the Honduran-Guatemalan border early, we had to wait until it opened, which was some time after seven in the morning. There was no problem, really, because we were on the shopping excursion bus. The tour leader charges a lot in order to pay off officials, both in Honduras and in Guatemala. The visa allows you to stay only a week or so, but the bribe is for Immigration. They know that some people aren't there just to shop, that some of them, like us, won't return. But they don't know which ones.

"When we reached Guatemala City, we went to the hotel where the other children had arrived a few days before. We asked for them at the front desk and learned that they had already gone. Their tour leader, though, was still there, and she reassured us by saying, 'Everything's fine. I took the children to the friend's house. She's a nice and caring woman.' Then she asked us where we planned to sleep.

" 'We're not acquainted with anything around here,' Marisa said.

" 'Don't worry. I'll talk to the man at the desk.'

"But Marisa had already asked and said, 'He says there's no room.'

" 'Don't worry. I'll find a place.' The woman had been running the tour for many years and had always brought people to that hotel. She trusted the man at the desk and had given him presents to show her appreciation. He, in turn, treated her and all her clients well. She went to him and said, 'Look, they can stay in my room or with people on my tour. I'll pay you a little more, but they'll stay here.'

"The people, whose rooms were full of merchandise after two days of shopping, were returning to Nicaragua the next day. I shared a room with a woman who used to be my neighbor in Estelí, so I sent a note back to Omar with her, assuring him that so far, all had gone well.

"The next day, we went to Leticia's friend's house where the rest of the family was waiting. Mundo called to tell us he'd pick us up early. We had to be at a bus stop by eight o'clock the following morning.

"We left Guatemala City with Uncle Mundo. I carried a bag containing one change of clothes for each of us: a blouse, pants, and underwear. 'We have to get moving. Walk fast. Let's go!' he yelled at us. We hurried to a bus stop and eventually took a bus that said 'Tecún Umán.' Meanwhile, Mundo warned us not to talk with anyone on the trip. Nothing, we should say nothing.

"We reached Tecún Umán on the Guatemalan-Mexican border around two or three o'clock that afternoon. It's a nice town, simple and pretty.[5] People use bicycles for taxis. The front has two wheels

---

[5]Five years later, Tecún Umán was described as a "squalid and bustling town" on what has become a "new border, where the line that divides Guatemala and Mexico now represents what the line between Mexico and the United States has been for decades—the gateway for the daring and lucky, the ultimate barrier for

with a wooden frame that seats four or five people and has a roof in case there's too much sun. The back, where the driver sits, has one wheel. The poor man drives by himself, sweating.

"The driver took us to a place where Coca-Cola is sold, and Mundo told us that while he was gone, we should drink our Cokes slowly. When he came back, he rushed us. 'Let's go. Let's go,' he said and again warned us not to talk. We took the taxi that looked like a bicycle again.

"Mundo told the driver to take us toward the Suchiate River. The ride frightened us because the taxi almost turned over. The streets aren't paved, so they're bumpy and dirty. Mundo told us that once a bicycle tipped over on his mother, sister, brother, and him. They fell on the dusty ground with the bike on top. After hearing that, we, of course, thought the same thing would happen to us, so we held on tightly. Just as we reached the river, we were about to fall.

"At the river, Mundo told us to act as if we were looking around and to pretend he wasn't with us. Since we rarely said anything out loud and instead communicated by small gestures and glances, he motioned for us to go to the group of people washing clothes on the river's edge and blend in with them.

"When we got there, a woman approached us, asking, 'Are you crossing to the other side?' I didn't want to talk, mainly because I was afraid of Mundo. I know the nature of the man, and so do the girls. He has a hard character and almost never smiles, always grumpy, irritable, and he fights with everyone. He annoys people. He's younger than Sergio, about thirty-five, I'd guess. Not a man you'd ever greet with a hug or kiss, but he does touch the children's faces.

"However, in spite of being afraid of him, I said yes to the woman, but added that we were with a relative. She whispered, 'Then watch out because *la migra*'s close by. They [Immigration officials] can catch you and take you up there, up to the prison. Be careful.' Then she went back to washing clothes and hanging them on rocks to dry, just like my mother used to do years ago in the Estelí River.

---

the frustrated." The city has become "an anarchic spot where life is as hard as it is cheap, where abandoned children sleep in the streets and furtive men and women cower in flophouses, waiting for contact from a smuggler." The population had doubled in the last decade. Tracy Wilkinson, "Dreams Die on Mexico's 2nd Border," *Los Angeles Times*, January 1, 1994.

"I was watching her bathe her daughter when Mundo approached. 'Wait for me here,' he whispered, 'and don't move. I'm going to the other side, to Mexico. I'll be back.' I think he went to see if he could arrange for us to cross the river, which people did by sitting on rafts made of wooden boards strapped on top of two inner tubes.

"We waited. After a while the woman turned to me and warned, 'Don't look back. *La migra*'s coming.'

" 'Right now?' Then I remembered that we were in Guatemala with Guatemalan visas and felt more secure, but since we did not have Mexican visas, I worried what *la migra* would think. They'd wonder for what possible reason would we be at the river's edge, between Guatemala and Mexico, close to where everybody crosses the border.

"The Immigration officer, dressed in his uniform, stopped us. 'What are you doing here?'

"Marisa answered. 'We're just looking around,' she said. 'We like it here, and my little sister is swimming.'

"I quickly added, 'That's true. We're waiting for her while she swims.'

" 'Your papers?' he asked.

"We showed him our papers. He checked them and gave them back. As he was leaving, he stopped a few yards away to talk with a man—they must know most people aren't there just to take a walk—and then he started to come back. By then, Mundo was already on a raft in the middle of the river, pushing and pulling it across.

"Mundo was hurrying, but the Immigration officer came back, took our passports, and told us that we had to go with him. Mundo was getting closer. I told the officer that if it was necessary for someone to go, I'd do it, but I first had to dry off and dress Nora. I was trying to stall him, trying to give Mundo time to cross the river.

"Mundo arrived while I was still dressing Nora. 'What happened?' he asked me.

" 'This man from Immigration said we had to show him our papers, our passports.'

" 'Don't move,' he mumbled. 'I'll take care of it. All he wants is money.'

"Mundo was right. He went to talk with the officer, gave him some money, and returned with our passports. We waited for a half hour, got on the raft, and crossed to the other side, to Mexico.

"The crossing itself was scary. The river is narrow but deep. Since we had to sit close to the edge of the raft, we all thought we'd fall in. Some people swam with the raft, pulling and pushing it. When we reached Mexico, we got off quickly, ran past the Immigration office, and once more got on bicycles that were taxis.

"The taxis took us to a place near a little town, maybe five blocks. We were standing there, looking around for anyone who might have followed us, when Mundo said, 'We have to leave. Walk. Run, if possible. Fast. I'm sure the taxi drivers went back to tell Immigration, and Immigration will come after us in a car.'

"We ran who-knows-how-many blocks. Then, on Mundo's orders, we dashed into a drugstore to hide, but he continued running. It was so awkward for all of us. We couldn't go outside because we were afraid, and we couldn't stay in the drugstore because we were embarrassed. People were shopping, so they were distracted, but once in a while they looked at us and wondered.

"Soon, Mundo pulled up in a taxi and motioned for us to run, to get in. We left quickly. After a few blocks, as we sped down the street, the taxi driver looked in his rearview mirror and yelled, 'Here comes *la migra*! They've seen us!' The official car pulled in front of us, signaling our driver to stop, which he did, and the Immigration officers' car stopped a little farther up the road. They called Mundo to their car and he went.

"We stayed seated in the taxi, so afraid. The driver said, 'If he has money, and if he gives it to them, it'll be all right. Here in Mexico everything can be arranged with money.' So we sat there waiting for Mundo to give them money. I don't know what Mundo and the Immigration officials talked about, but he offered them money—I don't know how much—and they took it and let us go. Mundo told the driver to take us to the train station, but as soon as the driver dropped us off and turned his car around, Mundo said, 'We have to run again. The driver could tell other people in Immigration, and then they'd come after us for money.'

"We ran again until we reached a hotel where there was a woman who seemed to be a friend of his. He told us to wait there and he'd be back. He returned an hour later, probably around eight o'clock, and said, 'Well, we'll have to stay here overnight. We can't leave today.' The woman found a place for us with one small bed and two bigger ones. Mundo said we had to get up early, but before we went to bed, he went shopping. He bought hot dogs and a Coke that we all shared. We bathed so that we'd relax and sleep all night.

"Around five o'clock in the morning, a taxi took us to a bus that took us to another bus, and then another, as usual. Around eight o'clock we got on a bus to I-don't-know-where. I didn't know if we were headed north, south, here, or there. Again, Mundo warned us that if we were stopped along the way, we were to give the name of the first town where we got on the bus. I don't even remember the name now. It was all too confusing. Sometimes we rode on the wrong buses and got off even more flustered.

"Immigration did stop the bus, though. No one on the bus was sleeping, except us, and we were just pretending. *¡Ay, dios mío!* I was trembling. And poor Miguel. He thought they'd take us to prison, maybe kill us, or never set us free. The officials came by, shined a flashlight in our eyes, but nothing happened.

"By the time we arrived in Mexico City, we had spent so much time in buses that we didn't know what day it was. I just remember it was dark, although it was morning. At first, I thought it was going to storm or rain, but it was just dark, cloudy, and polluted.

"Miguel—so pale—got off the bus and vomited. He hadn't eaten a thing, just a sip of water. This whole trip, the entire idea, frightened him. Once we stayed on the same bus for two days and nights, and he vomited often—mostly water—in the aisle.

"So there we were, in dark Mexico City. Miguel was sick, and we had a long walk ahead of us. Eventually we took a bus to a bus stop, but while we were waiting there, an Immigration car that looked like the police came by, and Mundo told us to say we were from Puebla. 'Where are you from?' they asked. Mundo told him and added, 'I'm traveling with my nieces and my sister-in-law. They're on vacation.' Another officer asked Mundo the same question and then asserted, 'I think you're a *coyote*.'

" 'Oh, no,' answered Mundo, and he showed him some papers. I don't know what they were or how he got them. The officers let us go, but they still seemed to be watching to see where we went or what we did. Mundo was aware of that so he said, 'Let's walk straight ahead, without looking around. We have to walk and walk fast.' He took us to another bus stop, but the men were still behind us. Mundo made us go down some stairs, places you go down to catch a bus, then come back up, still walking fast and not turning around. 'If you look back, they'll know you're not from here,' Mundo warned. We took a bus that stopped near Mundo's home. I don't know how I managed to get there. I was almost dead, and so was Miguel.

"It hadn't seemed dangerous to me until we crossed into Mexico. The problem was that everyone knows how Nicaraguans speak, and in Mexico, most of us are illegal. If many Nicaraguans move there, Mexicans will be out of work, and Nicaraguans will be hired because employers pay us less; and since we don't know the laws concerning benefits and we're illegal, they pay us whatever they want.

"Mundo's place is small. There's room for two small beds along the walls, and in the center, a small semicircular sofa, a television set, and a small table. His sister, wife, and son live with him, and they told us we could make whatever food we wanted. They had everything: beans, bread, rice, eggs. But who wanted to eat then? No one. We just wanted to rest.

"The neighbor came, a humble woman who had an equally humble apartment, and invited us to sleep with her because she had fewer people at her place. We ended up spending most of our time there. Mundo's wife worked and he was to take care of their child, and sometimes he did, but he was a man who didn't know how to change a child's diapers or how to give the baby medicine. I don't know why men become so useless, but I said to him, 'Look, this is how to put on a diaper, here is the medicine, this is how to rock the child.' That's how I ended up taking care of the child.

"Actually, Mundo and I got along well. Instead of criticizing Miguel or the girls, he said, 'Look, tell the children this-and-that thing,' but he never got himself involved. That was fine. But one day I was gone, and when I returned the baby was crying. Sofía was in the bathroom, and when she came out, he began to treat her poorly, vulgarly, with dirty words—words that men use when they fight. He said, '*Sos más grande boluda, una hija de puta*'[6] (You're the most lazy good-for-nothing person and a daughter of a whore).

"So Sofía yelled back and said, 'I've respected you because you're my uncle. But you don't deserve our respect because you're making money on us. You've no right to hit us, yell at us, or treat us poorly because my mother and dad pay you for everything we eat. If you don't want to take us to the States, then tell our father and he'll send someone else. We don't have to put up with this.'

---

[6]There are many definitions for *boluda*, but in this case it was meant to say she was lazy. Since *boluda* can be considered to be a synonym for *huevona*, especially in Central America, and refers to testicles, the word was so vulgar that Yamileth was reluctant to repeat it. *Hija de puta* is literally "daughter of a whore."

And she left for the other apartment. She didn't return that day or the next.

"Later he said to me, 'I'm nervous here, of what I'm not sure,' looking for justification. I said, 'Look, if you're nervous, why do you agree to take people across the border, especially if you think you're not going to be able to do it? A person so nervous shouldn't be involved with things like this.' Only at certain times, he said, did he lose control, but he always seemed like that to me. In Mexico, he always acted as if he were hiding."

~

"We were invited to spend Christmas with Rocío, a sister of Mundo and Sergio's, but Mundo didn't come with us. We've always known, ever since Sergio married Leticia, that almost everyone in that family believes they're better than others, and especially better than our family. Even though they have nothing, they think they belong to a higher social class, so I don't like most of them. When I realized the invitation was for dinner, I didn't want to stay because I didn't feel comfortable being in their house, knowing how they feel about us. When Rocío wanted everyone to try her Nicaraguan tamales called *nacatamales*[7]—she said they were very good—I didn't go into the living room where everyone was eating them. When her daughter's rich boyfriend arrived with his mother, I didn't go out to meet them, either. I said I was sick and didn't want to eat. They brought me a drink in the room where I was watching television with Miguel and Nora.

"Then the rich boyfriend and his mother invited us all to their house. I said I couldn't because I was sick, so I asked if I could stay and watch television. Rocío said no one was allowed to stay, everyone had to go, so we all went. The rich boyfriend's house was big with all the comforts and luxuries possible. They had several cars and owned many stores. On a large table were all sorts of fruit, food, nuts. The family had paintings and framed currency from other countries on the walls and a crèche.

"Miguel and the other boys wanted to play bingo. I stayed with them pretending to enjoy the game so that I didn't have to sit with the others, but they called me and I had to go and have some wine and nuts. The rich boyfriend's mother said we were to take part in a *posada*. That's when you walk around the house carrying the

---

[7]Made of pork, raisins, rice, and potatoes covered with corn flour dough, they were wrapped in a banana leaf and cooked for an hour in a double boiler.

crèche and everyone has candles and sings songs. People behind a closed door sing to ask permission to enter with the Baby Jesus. We do it in Nicaragua but not in the house. We do it in a barrio, a neighborhood, but rarely in Estelí because it's more of a small-town tradition. You give sweet rolls and coffee to the people who bring the Baby Jesus. When they go, they leave the Baby Jesus behind for that family to take to another house.

"After the *posada*, they gave us sparklers and then the rich boy-friend said, 'Now let's break the *piñatas*,' so we did. They had fruit inside! In Nicaragua we have lollipops, sweets covered in wrappers, but no fruit. Miguel was surprised to see fruit, sugarcane, and peanuts. After that, it was time for dinner because it was midnight.

"When the food was on the table, the rich boyfriend's mother said that we all had to say some words of gratitude for the day, and she gave everyone—there were twenty-four of us at one big table—a glass of champagne. The woman toasted us and thanked us for agreeing to celebrate Christmas with them. She said they were proud to have a Nicaraguan family in their home and offered to help us anytime in the future if we needed a friend.

"I thanked them for sharing their dinner with us and making us feel part of their family, which they had, and I thanked them for the opportunity to be with them. I also said I was sad to be far away from my land and not to have my mother with me, who had died a year ago that month.

"The children said, 'Thank you for having us,' nothing more. Everyone started to cry, but the husband said, 'No, let's not cry. We should be happy because this is an important day, the day of God's birth.' We toasted after each person spoke, and when the glasses were empty, they were filled up again. Everyone applauded the toast, laughed, and we ate whatever we wanted. I ate some guacamole and bread, and they called on me to say something more. Then they gave us some kind of *atole* [a drink made from corn flour] and sherbet for the children. Later they gave us some tea—so awful tasting—with honey and a piece of cinnamon stick. This was around two in the morning, so we were sleepy, but we didn't get to bed until three.

"The following morning at nine o'clock, the boyfriend and his family took us to the Shrine of the Virgin of Guadalupe because they wanted us to have good memories of Mexico. After that, we went to Chapultepec, where there are crazy games, like roller coasters and bumper cars. Miguel loved the bumper cars, but I didn't go on any rides. My stomach wasn't feeling so good. Miguel went on more rides, and I asked for an Alka-Seltzer. The family paid for everything and returned us to Mundo around seven o'clock that night. We all went right to bed. By then everyone, especially those who had gone on the rides, was sick.

"The day Mundo told us to leave, we left. The six of us and Mundo traveled by bus for probably the next two or three days. We went through many towns, but I don't remember the names. There was a bathroom on the bus—the first time I had seen such a vehicle. I knew a plane had one, but a bus? Miguel whispered, 'I'm sick, and I'm afraid that. . . .'

" 'Look what it says there. This bus has a bathroom.'

" 'You think so?'

" 'Yes, *hombre*!' I answered, 'Let's go.'

"We locked ourselves in, and he vomited. A *señora* who was seated nearby saw us go in and saw how bad Miguel looked. She could also hear him vomiting. When we left, she handed me a little white pill for Miguel. He took it and felt better. I think it was a pill to help people who get sick in a moving vehicle. Afterward, Miguel asked me why I hadn't asked the woman the name of the pill, but I said it was better that we not say anything, that we not speak.

"We got off somewhere near Tijuana. Mundo bought some tacos, but no one wanted any. He's a big eater, so he ate them. We took another bus to Tijuana, and then another one to a place near the border crossing. We arrived at a hotel around four o'clock in the afternoon, and Mundo got Cokes and bread for us. I don't remember if we ate anything besides the bread, but I do remember that I tried to eat a little more so that I could sleep. Sometimes when you're afraid and your stomach's empty, it's hard to sleep.

"Mundo was afraid, I was afraid, everyone was afraid. Mundo said we'd cross early the next morning.

"We left somewhere between six and half past. We took a taxi for fifteen or twenty minutes. Mundo warned us and said, 'As soon as the taxi stops, get out quickly, and follow me.' The taxi stopped, and Mundo got out and went through an opening in the chain-link fence that divides Mexico from the United States. Beyond the fence is a riverbed, and beyond that, up a little higher, is a road where the Immigration vehicles go back and forth, making sure that no one gets across. We were tired of the cold. The entire trip had been horribly cold, but it was worse at the border, near the riverbed. There I saw lots of people. I turned to Mundo and asked, 'Are all these people going to cross?'

" 'Many are,' he said, 'but some are just watching.'

"There must have been twenty to twenty-five people just where we were, and even more farther on. In the riverbed we saw, near a stream of dirty water, lots of empty cartons and bags. But we also saw a dead man, or it could have been a woman. No one paid any attention to the body. It seemed to be a common occurrence.

"Mundo said we'd have to wait, maybe until after four o'clock in the afternoon, because there were so many people there and that made him worry that we might be beaten, killed, or robbed. While he was explaining that to me, we saw the Immigration patrol crossing from one place to another. We hid in the riverbed, and Mundo said that when he signaled us, we should run as fast as we could. The vehicle passed by. Some people ran across, but the vehicle turned around and went after them, so we ran back as far as we had come. We spent the next two or three hours running up, then going back, up and back."

Three

The North Is Different from the Postcards

—I felt my batteries go low.

No one even glanced at the dead body lying in the middle of the nearly dry riverbed. Their eyes, instead, followed the cruising border patrol van, back and forth, back and forth, on the highway beyond the arroyo. They watched and waited for two or three hours. The change of clothes they had brought from Nicaragua had been discarded; they had earlier tucked any small memento of their old life into their pockets or underwear. Suddenly, Uncle Mundo yelled, "Go! Run!" It was time. There was no turning back. They ran—jumping over small ditches, passing the body—and crossed to the other side of the border. Yamileth and her family had arrived in the United States.

"Uncle Mundo called a taxi from a woman's house, and an hour later we were in a San Diego park. It must have been around noon because people were having lunch. A friend of ours in the United States, Ken Bunker, had arranged for his friend Alan to pick us up.[1] We stood at a bus stop while Mundo called him. Alan said he'd be there in two hours. It was January 1, 1989, but none of us knew that. Maybe Mundo knew, but the rest of us were confused about the time, day, everything.

---

[1]Ken Bunker, a schoolteacher from California and Oregon, had studied Spanish in Estelí for a few weeks during which time he lived at Leticia's home. After he came back to the United States, he returned to Nicaragua to visit the family. Through the years, he maintained close contact with them. He died in 1994 while hiking on Mount Adams in the state of Washington.

"While we waited at the bus stop, we saw so many crazy people in the park. Some played music by hitting tin cans with wooden sticks, others talked on the phone with the receiver backwards, some rifled through the garbage, and others yelled at each other. I laughed. Lots of crazy people in that place.

"We sat on a bench nearby as if we were waiting for a bus. The problem was we didn't know what Alan or his car looked like, and Mundo had forgotten to ask. Whenever a car came by that looked like it could be Alan's, we all waved, looking just like the rest of the crazy people in the park. Finally, one of the drivers pulled up and smiled at us. Mundo went up to him and asked for his name. It was Ken's friend. As we settled into his car, we said to each other, '¡Dios mío! What a relief!' Mundo asked to be dropped off near the train station, and we said good-bye. 'See you later,' he replied and went back to Mexico.

"Alan took us to his home where Sergio, the girls' father, was to pick us up. What I remember most about Alan is that his wife offered us some apples to eat. We grabbed them, one for each of us, and started to eat them as if we were thirsty. It embarrassed us to be dripping wet with apple juice, so we went to the patio. We were like little children quickly devouring stolen apples.

"Sergio arrived an hour and a half later. It had been nearly two years since Sergio had seen his daughters. He had forgotten their ages and didn't know the dates of their birthdays, so he said to each one, 'How old are you? Oh, so grown up!' He didn't keep up with their ages, their birthdays, that sort of thing, as other fathers do. He didn't live for his family. It's hard to understand, but each person's head is a world unto its own. He wasn't particularly affectionate with me or with my son since we've never had much in common.

"He drove us to Los Angeles. I didn't expect the city to look like that. I had seen postcards that people sent to Nicaragua. Some of them had tall buildings with beautiful lights and the card said 'New York,' so I thought all cities, no matter what they were called, looked like that. But Los Angeles wasn't like that at all. Even though Miguel and I hadn't talked about it beforehand, both of us had seen the postcards, so he, too, was surprised.

"Sergio's whole family—mother, brothers, sisters—and Leticia were waiting for us in an apartment. We were relieved and happy to finally be there. Leticia was emotional, crying and hugging us. She'd been afraid that something would happen to us in the crossing, as has happened to many people. But there we were. We all made it."

I had known that Yamileth, her thirteen-year-old son Miguel, and Leticia's daughters might try to come to the United States, but dates were vague, and for all I knew, they might even have decided against the trip. On New Year's Day, 1989, Leticia called from Los Angeles, her voice heavy with sadness, as it often was. I asked what was wrong. She told me that indeed the family had left Nicaragua, but that was a few weeks ago; she had heard nothing from them and was worried that they had met with some disaster. I remember feeling scared and helpless. How could I find out what had happened to them somewhere between Nicaragua and Los Angeles? I listened as her mournful voice failed to answer my insistent questions.

Suddenly, laughter and yelling screeched over the phone. Soon I was talking with an exuberant Yamileth. It took me a few seconds to shake off my concern and realize that I had been tricked. They had arrived safely and decided to play a joke on me. Doña María would have been proud of her daughters' mischievous humor. They laughed and laughed, and I, who moments before had imagined the worst, was speechless and relieved.

They arrived in Los Angeles just as the economy was starting on a downturn and jobs were becoming scarce; nonetheless, the myth of the city held out hope for them. Yamileth had expected to find Los Angeles full of opportunities for those who were willing to work hard. Instead, the family watched the city become a hard-luck place where taxpayers claimed that they could no longer afford to support all of the welfare recipients and where gangs murdered so often that the killings received little attention in the media.

Yamileth and her immigrant family were not alone: 1989 was one of the years when the numbers of undocumented immigrants soared in California.[2] Latinos made up 40 percent of the population, José was the most common name that parents gave their infant sons, and long ago salsa had outsold catsup. Most Central Americans who arrived in Los Angeles in the 1980s ended up in South-Central Los Angeles, in the nearby and smaller Pico-Union neighborhood, or in the surrounding areas near the city's center. In the last twenty-five years, many of those neighborhoods have gone from mostly African-American to over half Latino, making them the first stop for many, like Yamileth, in their search for a respite from the wars and poverty in their native lands.

---

[2]Jaime Olivares, "Campaña antiinmigrante influirá en elecciones de 1994," *La Opinión* (Los Angeles), August 16, 1993.

The family's first apartment was just west of MacArthur Park, in the middle of a community that Yamileth described as Latino but English-speaking. Even though Yamileth had known that she should not believe all of the wondrous stories about life in the United States, she had believed some of them. Without her realizing it, she had imagined Leticia living well—not luxuriously, but certainly better than she had in Nicaragua. Nothing had prepared her for what she saw.

"Sergio's mother offered us something to eat, but I didn't want anything because at that moment, I didn't understand the situation. All I wanted was an Alka-Seltzer. The problem was that I didn't know if Sergio and Leticia had their own apartment or not. I knew Leticia didn't like to live with Sergio's family since they've never gotten along well, so it seemed strange to me from the very moment I saw all of them in that one-room apartment. Maybe they had just gotten together for our arrival. I simply didn't know. It hadn't occurred to me that they all, including Sergio's two brothers, two sisters, and mother, lived in one room.

"Imagine my surprise when I heard the apartment house manager, Sergio's sister Lupe, say that there was an apartment to rent. We simply didn't understand. Where did Leticia and Sergio live? Where were we going to live? Miguel had come with all sorts of dreams, illusions, and so had the girls. All of us had our own imagined world in our heads, an image different from what was in front of us.

"Around ten o'clock at night, when it was time to go to bed, Leticia took some clothes and blankets out of the closet. She handed the blankets to the children, packed some clothes in a big suitcase, and we left for an apartment. I didn't even realize it was the empty one that Lupe had earlier mentioned. I thought Leticia and Sergio had already been living in an apartment, that they were established there, but when we opened the door, *¡Dios mío!* What a shock!

"The apartment was like a single drawer, as we say, *un solo cajón*, just a tiny box of a room that had a bathroom, a closet, and a kitchen along the wall. There was no furniture, no bed, nothing. It wasn't possible to divide the room, either. If you made a bedroom, there was no living room, and if you made a living room, there was no bedroom. It was so small and cost four hundred fifty dollars a month. Just looking at it, as we say in Nicaragua, I felt my batteries go low. I was demoralized, without the strength to go on, and with the urge to cry.

"Leticia couldn't explain it. She tried, but for me it was too much of a surprise. Miguel gestured, showing that he was as astounded as I was. The apartment didn't matter to the girls, and really not to me, either, but the lie mattered. What we had been told, the lie, was the biggest surprise.

"I didn't tell Miguel, but I thought about how I had my bed in Nicaragua, I had my room, my house where Miguel could shout and play with the boys in the little yard. There we could talk with our neighbors, but here, no, there was nothing. Miguel couldn't play because Sergio wouldn't let him go outside and didn't want him to disturb the neighbors. You always had to be quiet, go down the stairs quietly, go up again quietly. It was like when you want to sing a happy song and you can't because it bothers the people next door.

"Sergio went back to his mother's to get his television set and borrow a table and some mattresses. That night he used one to sleep on and two of the girls had the other. Leticia and the other two girls slept on clothes they laid out on the carpet. Miguel and I slept on clothes on the closet floor, where at least we had our privacy.

"Miguel whispered to me, 'Is this how *Tía* Leticia lives?' I said yes, but I still couldn't believe it. He added, 'We'll see what they tell us tomorrow,' and we went to sleep.

"We slept like rocks and got up late. Then we realized that we had nothing to cook and nothing to cook in. I didn't know the prices or how to shop, so Sergio brought us milk, bread, and butter while Leticia talked with us. She asked how Mundo had treated us, and the girls told her about themselves. She said her work wasn't good, and Sergio's job at a juice factory didn't pay well.

"Sergio's family lent us a pot to cook beans in, one to make rice, and another for meat, and two glasses, and Sergio bought beans, rice, chicken, cooking oil, and also flour to make corn tortillas. I made some beans and the girls helped me make the chicken. More than anything, I wanted my beans with rice and tortillas. That's how we spent the first day in the United States.

"On Monday, Sergio went to work early in the morning, and Marisa, who didn't like housework, decided to go with her mother to the salon. I explained to Leticia that, given the situation and the disorder we were in, Marisa—who I mistakenly thought was going to go to school—could go with her that day, but the next day was another matter. The children had to be registered in school, and there was much to do.

"I asked Lupe how to register the children—neither Leticia nor Sergio had time to do it—and she agreed to go with me the next day. I took the ages of the children with me: Nora was eight, Miguel eleven,[3] Chela fifteen, Sofía almost seventeen, and Marisa around eighteen. I really didn't care if Miguel went to school or not. On the one hand, I'd like it so he would meet other children, but on the other, they say everyone speaks English, which means he wouldn't understand. Besides, we'd be returning to Nicaragua soon.

"At the school, a woman asked me in Spanish for their vaccination documents. I had nothing, nothing. I told her we hadn't been here long. She gave me a ten o'clock appointment at a health center. The place was, of course, totally unknown to me.[4] When she used the word "appointment," I thought that meant I had a set appointment for ten o'clock. I had no idea I'd be at the health center the entire day. For breakfast, we ate just a little bread with milk and weren't prepared to last all day. By noon we were dying of hunger, but we had no money. The children had to fill out forms, answer questions, wait, get the vaccinations, wait, take a Spanish test, and take another one by describing the countryside, what they saw there, all kinds of things.

"As we were filling out the forms, I realized that Leticia had to sign some of them. Although it was her day off, I had gone with the children so she could rest. Fortunately, I'd taken Sergio's mother's telephone number, so I called Leticia. She came at half past two, signed the papers—which was all she had to do—and still it took us two hours more to get out of there.

"It was a long walk home. Even though Sergio got home early that day and could have picked us up, he didn't, which irritated Leticia. On top of that, we got back to the apartment, starving after the two-hour walk, only to discover that there was no food. No one had bothered cooking. I tried to make something but my head hurt too much. I was so disappointed and tried to lie down for a while. I was worn out with hunger. I went to the closet to rest.

"A few days later, we returned to the health center—back through the streets for the two-hour walk with the troop of chil-

---

[3]Miguel was actually thirteen, but his passport said eleven, so Yamileth gave that age.

[4]It was the H. Claude Hudson Comprehensive Health Care Center.

dren—to have the vaccination checked. I warned the children to eat enough because surely it would take a long time. I was right.

"So the vaccinations were done, but that day I learned of another problem. Chela was to go to one school, Sofía to another, and both Miguel and Nora to Magnolia School. I knew where Magnolia was, but Sofía's school was far away. She had to go by bus to a school located on boulevard I-don't-know-what, street I-don't-know-where. It was the same situation with Chela's school, a place called Berendo. Since Lupe knew a little about addresses, I asked her how to get there. She told me to walk three blocks, ask questions, and pay attention to the street signs. The problem was English. After the three blocks, I showed the address to a person who motioned for me to continue straight ahead, which I did for seven blocks, and then I stopped another person, who sent me another two blocks, on and on until I reached the school. At each corner I stopped and drew on the map—nothing pretty, but enough to find my way back. When I finally got there, students weren't being registered that day! I soon saw how I could spend the whole day doing something and accomplishing nothing.

"I went back to the apartment to get Sofía's papers, thinking I could register her and make something out of my day. Sergio was there, so I asked him where the school was, but he said we'd have to wait for Leticia. ¡Ay, Dios mío! When Leticia came in, I angrily told her, 'Listen, I've tried to do what I could, but if you don't do your share, the girls aren't going to school. I'm trying hard, but I'm not familiar with things here. I have no idea what to do. I meet people on the street and can't ask them anything because they speak only English. You've been here longer. You know what to do and I don't.' I was really disgusted. Leticia helped after that.

"Sofía took the bus to Canoga Park High School—hours away in the San Fernando Valley. Chela, once I showed her the way, could walk to school. The two young ones didn't want to stay in school. The first day, they said they understood nothing. It was all in English. Same thing the second day and the third. In Miguel's class, one other student spoke Spanish. Nora said everyone spoke only English in her class, but that might have been her way of protesting. Maybe the other children had been here long enough to learn English.

"One of the teachers, along with a translator, gave an assignment to Miguel in Spanish. He was to tell a story about a boy who wanted to fly a helicopter. He told me his ideas, and I took notes, and he wrote the story in his notebook. He liked that, but once back in school, the class was in English. He was confused. He couldn't understand. He thought he'd start with numbers or simple words like 'pencil,' 'blackboard,' 'chalk,' small things he could be shown and then learn to say. I told him to be patient because we still didn't know what the classes would be like.

"A week after he started school, he developed a high fever and a pain in the arm that had been vaccinated. I took him back to the health center where I was advised to keep him home so that the germs in the classroom didn't make him get worse. They gave me a note for the school nurse saying he'd be out for two weeks.**"**

Late in January, I sent Yamileth and Miguel train tickets to Oregon. They were anxious to visit, and it was a good time for us to have them as guests in our home. They had been in the United States for less than a month.

"Miguel and I were desperate to leave Los Angeles. Just as we were ready to leave, I got sick with the flu, a little fever, and I also thought that since I was having intense pain with my period, one or two of my ovaries were inflamed. Actually, I think I was sick of being locked up in that apartment. Leticia said I was too sick to go, canceled the reservation, and made a new one, but Miguel was impatient and said, 'Take a pill. Get better, and let's go. Don't be afraid that we'll get lost. I'm sure they live close by.'

" 'No,' I said, 'they say that we won't arrive until the next day.'

" 'Well,' he reassured me, 'it won't be bad because we'll have a place to sit.'

"There was no one to take us to the train the day we left. Everyone had to work or their cars weren't running. 'Oh, don't worry, by asking you can get anywhere,' I told them. 'You just need a little patience.'

"I told Leticia we'd go early in the morning—we had to be there by nine o'clock—to allow ourselves enough time to ask along the way. So we got up early, and Leticia called in Spanish to find out where to catch the bus to the station. She walked us there and gave me twelve or thirteen dollars to use for the bus and for food on the train.

"We got on the bus. The driver didn't speak Spanish, so I handed him this little folded piece of paper with the address of the station. He was trying to tell me it was the wrong bus, but I didn't understand. We got another bus, and even though the driver spoke Spanish, it was the wrong bus, too. He took us to another bus that took us part of the way.

"After that, we ran. It was getting late, and I knew we were going to miss the train. We crossed the street, avoiding the people who looked like drug addicts and making sure they didn't follow us. We kept running. One person told me the station was in one direction, but I was careful and asked another, who told me the opposite direction. Finally, a group of women told us we were running in the right direction, just three or four blocks more. I had seen the station once before, so I knew if I saw something like a church, like a cathedral, we'd be there.

"We arrived at half past nine. Could we still catch the train? 'No problem,' the agent said. He got our tickets ready and told us to run. I kept saying, 'But where, where? I don't know where!' He called to another man who was going in the same direction and he helped us. A woman was taking tickets at the train, and that same man translated for us and told her that we were going to Oregon and that we didn't speak English. The man even put us on the train.

"Once inside we didn't know where to sit, if we should go to another car, or what we should do. We just stopped. Along came a young man who told Miguel to sit in one place and me in another, separate from each other.

"The train started. Miguel, still confident that you lived close to Los Angeles, said, 'We'll be getting off in just a little while.' He sat with a young man who didn't speak Spanish, and I with an older woman who didn't, either. She was making things out of wool and talked to me in English. I just smiled because I didn't have any idea what she was saying. Lots of announcements were made on the loudspeaker, but I didn't understand. I had the letter you gave me in case anything went wrong.[5] Even I started to hope that Oregon was close.

"They handed out one of those map-like papers telling where the train went, the hours, prices, and the list of food, but I understood nothing. The woman asked me if I was going to have breakfast or lunch, whatever it is you eat between ten and eleven o'clock. Since I didn't know how to order, I said no. On one of the papers, I saw the words "hot dog" and the price, around two dollars. Miguel,

---

[5] I had sent them a letter in English that they were to use if needed; it explained where they were going and how to contact me if there were any difficulties during the journey.

by gesturing to the young man next to him, found out that one Coca-Cola cost seventy-five cents. We gave the man the money, and he brought a Coke back for each of us.

"Later we got braver. We tried to find where the food was sold. The train was long, four cars, but we found it and managed to order two hot dogs and two Cokes. The problem was the bathroom. We wanted to use it, but both of us were afraid and embarrassed because we didn't know how. '¡*Híjole!*[6] I'm going to ask,' I told him. 'I don't know how I'm going to do it, but I'm going to find out. Wait here.' But he didn't want to wait alone. 'Stay here,' I repeated. 'Nothing will happen to you. I'll be right back.'

"When I found the bathroom, I was afraid to lock the door because I couldn't figure out the lock. I asked myself, 'What if I lock myself inside?' I had to urinate, so I went to get Miguel. I said, 'You go, Miguel, and I'll go with you.' I didn't tell him I was afraid I'd lock myself in. Sometimes it's easier for him to figure out these things. We found where it said 'Men,' and before he went in, he tried the lock and figured it out. And I watched and learned. I didn't ever tell him that I had been afraid I'd lock myself in."

---

[6]*Híjole* is a Spanish word—archaic in Spain but current in Mexico—that expresses surprise, wonder, or disgust, depending on the tone of voice. Yamileth started using the expression after she arrived in Los Angeles, probably as a result of being around the Spanish spoken by Mexican immigrants.

Four

Bathtubs and Beds in Oregon

—The bathtubs were like pools, and the beds were big.

"We were tired when we caught the train, so after a while we went to sleep. Suddenly, it got light outside, and we noticed that it was 'white white' everywhere. 'Wow,' said Miguel, 'what could that be?'

" 'Shhh, I think that's snow,' I answered. It was the first time we'd seen snow, so beautiful, just as we had imagined it to be.

" 'Will the train be able to go through with snow on the tracks?' Miguel asked. We had earlier seen a movie where people knocked snow down from trees, and we wanted to see the snow on trees for ourselves. When we did, Miguel said, 'Poor trees, they're going to die.' Just watching it snow gave me chills, just like when you have a cold, but we loved it."

It was January 29, 1989. George Bush had been inaugurated president a few days before, and the Sandinistas were desperately hanging on to power in Nicaragua as their economy spiraled downward. A cold wind blew across the Oregon station platform as the train pulled in. We looked up at the windows, hoping to see Yamileth and Miguel so we could motion for them to get off. No sign of them. Suddenly, they were jumping off the train, a laughing mother and son, looking small and childlike in their thin sweaters. We reached out to hug them, feeling as if our arms extended across the long distance between Oregon and Nicaragua.

Once settled in a daughter's bedroom in our Corvallis home, Yamileth and Miguel amused us with their stories about the train: the race to the station, the bathrooms, and the hot dogs. They brought us up to date on family members, and we talked about our mutual

friend Ken, how he had moved to Oregon, and their plans to see
him.

We rejoiced in seeing our culture through their eyes. Their insight and humor saved what could have been embarrassing moments. One day we were talking with them about our cat and how
she died, in an animal clinic. When Yamileth and Miguel heard
that, they looked at each other and both burst out laughing. Soon
we all were laughing about how ridiculous an animal clinic seemed
from a Nicaraguan perspective. Yamileth said, "You give priority
to animals and worry so much about them that they have clinics?
¡A la púchica!¹ A clinic for animals!"

The language also confused them. It all looked backward to
Yamileth. She puzzled: "In English, what goes behind is put in front.
For example, your daughters' old elementary school is Hoover
School, but everything is the reverse, and I don't know how to read
it. When I see a sign, I need to decipher it. First, I look at the end so
that I can understand it. First 'School' and then 'Hoover.' "

In Estelí, I had told them that our house was nice, but not a
mansion. But in Spanish, *mansión* conjures up a smaller home than
it does in English. No, it is not a mansion, but to Yamileth and
Miguel, newly arrived from the hilly tobacco area of Nicaragua, it
clearly seemed to be. As she said, "We imagined that you lived in
the countryside, which you do, and that the house was small, which
it's not. The bedroom surprised us even more. When we closed the
door behind us, Miguel said, 'This is so much better than Leticia's!
We're living like kings!' And we both laughed with joy. We were
so happy to be there. We thought of the stories we'd have to tell
when we returned to Nicaragua." To them, in Oregon, "the bathtubs were like pools, and the beds were big."

We also discussed pseudonyms, which I had so carefully used
throughout the 1980s, at their request, to protect them: Yamileth
liked hers (Marta), so she wanted to keep it while she was in the
United States, but Miguel, not liking his, asked to be called by his
real name.

If anyone in Oregon inquired, Yamileth was to say that she came
from Mexico, which is how she entered our country, but that skirted

---

¹*A la púchica* is a euphemism for *a la puta* (whore), which is short for *a la*
gran puta, a Central American expression of surprise or dismay, depending on
the context. This softened version is used among friends but not in more formal
situations. It could be translated as "I'll be damned!" or, more politely, as "I'll be
darned!"

the fact that she was Nicaraguan. As if Oregon wanted to dazzle them, the sky dumped several feet of snow on us. It was the biggest storm in our memory.

**"When it snowed at your house, we got to knock the snow out of the trees, just as we had seen in that movie. We got on the sled—Miguel was the driver—and slid down the hill and around the corner. It made me laugh and feel good because we had never seen snow or enjoyed one second of it. Being where there's snow is great! And then sliding down your hill, Miguel and I on the sled with the dog racing beside us, we felt so good. It made us laugh and laugh. When we returned to Los Angeles, Miguel boasted to the girls about the big snowman we made. Later, when we visited Ken in Hood River, it also snowed, and we crossed a frozen river.

"In Corvallis, we went to the Corvallis Clinic, not that we were sick, but in my country we don't even know what illnesses we have. We had a thorough exam in which they discovered that Miguel had every kind of parasite possible. We were surprised because we didn't know he was walking around with so much in him, but the medicine took care of the little animals, as we say, in his stomach. And it was the first time I had a gynecological exam. That was, for me, a difficult experience, even harder than driving in Los Angeles.[2] How I perspired! And how embarrassing to have the woman doctor see me. But I had no serious problems."**

The first long conversation that Yamileth and I had in Oregon was about her mother. Yamileth cried throughout the telling. She believed that on the anniversary of someone's death, you should pray all night long to mark the date. But a year after her mother's death, she and her son were somewhere south of Mexico City with Uncle Mundo.

After her mother's death, Yamileth began to have strange dreams and to imagine that someone was outside the front door of the house. She would go quietly to the door, open it, but see no one. Her friends in Estelí suggested ways to forget her problems, but nothing worked. She cried all the time and became so nervous that she went to the hospital for pills. Not a night went by that she did not dream.

---

[2]Yamileth and her family drove in Los Angeles. None of them, with the exception of Sergio, had driven often in Nicaragua, and they had not obtained licenses there. No one had a license in California, either, but all the adults drove, even on the freeways. The family had an unregistered and uninsured car in Los Angeles that they had bought from a relative.

Her dream was that her mother had been buried alive. Her mother could not open her eyes, but she could hear. Yamileth had been told, years ago during the literacy brigade,[3] of a student who had been teaching *campesinos* to read. Something happened to his heart—she did not know what—and he died. Two days later, when the *campesinos* were praying over his casket, the student must have heard them because he sat up and pushed open the box. Everyone in the room ran out except his girlfriend, who was "courageously" waiting for him in the candlelit room. Yamileth did not understand the medical words used to describe the incident, but she knew that he would have suffocated had they buried him. That must have happened to her mother, she said; that is what the dreams meant.

Furthermore, she talked with her mother, normally, as they always had. Her mother would say, "They came by to get you but couldn't find you. They left you something, though." Yamileth thought that "they" were looking into her life through her windows and doors. She knew that no one was there, but still she looked.

As she told me about her dreams about her mother, I regretted that only the day before I had told her that I had her mother's voice on all those tapes and asked her if she wanted to listen to them. I now remembered the silent no, the quick shake of her head.

"I always dream of her alive. I never dream of her going through the agony of the hospital. There she didn't speak, didn't open her eyes. Instead, I dream of her talking. There's not a day that goes by, not in Nicaragua, not in Oregon, not anywhere I go, that I don't dream about her. Sometimes the dreams frighten me, but other times they make me happy, as if I were sitting outside the house with her, laughing and talking. And some dreams leave me confused, dreams where she says to me, 'Don't go. Don't go far away. Make sure you return soon.' So I tell her that I'm not going to go, and she says, 'Good.' Then I ask, 'Mama, did you really think I'd leave?'

"At the same time, I know my mother's dead. In the same dream I say so, but then I say she's alive. I wake up in the morning with this horrible headache. She's alive, she's dead. But if she's dead, how could she be talking to me? Sometimes it's as if she were alive, doing things in my house, and I left her there all by herself.

---

[3]Soon after the 1979 Sandinista victory, a literacy brigade was created in which Nicaraguan students went into the countryside to teach *campesinos* how to read. Highly acclaimed, it dramatically increased literacy in Nicaragua.

"Last night I dreamed she was sick. She was lying down, and we were talking. Suddenly, someone said to me, 'Your mother's very sick,' and I told this person that I'd already given her the medicine. But this person said, 'You have to take her to the doctor,' but I said, 'No, she doesn't want to go.' Then I saw my mother sitting up and talking, and another part of the dream started.

"All the things that have happened to me since she died, since I left home, haven't been a big enough obstacle to stop the dreams. I'll dream all my life."

Ken Bunker had looked for a way for Yamileth and Miguel to stay in Oregon. A couple, Penny and Mark, who were good friends of his, had agreed to provide her room, board, and a small stipend in exchange for light housekeeping and child care, the kind of job Yamileth had done much of her life. Three days before she and Miguel were to leave for the new job, on February 23, I left the house with my seventeen-year-old daughter Megan, loudly complaining about the breast biopsy I was to have and promising to return in an hour or so. Megan would bring me home and go on to school afterward; I, rather than going to the university, had work that I could do at home.

I came back two hours later feeling like a pale stick figure wrapped in a trench coat. I could see myself only from the outside because the inside had shut down. The biopsy showed cancer. The nightmare began, all witnessed by wide-eyed and horrified Yamileth and Miguel. Spanish, which we had been speaking in order to include our guests, disappeared from the house; it was English from then on.

I went to bed. Tom came home, and he and Megan called our daughters Lisa and Heather, my mother, my brothers, our friends, and my department chair. I cried; everyone else was in shock and denial. I lay there, trying to let it sink in. Cancer. I did everything right. I ate right, exercised, was thin. So maybe I ate too many potato chips, but cancer? It will be all right, everyone said, but I was not so sure. Neither were Yamileth and Miguel.

They knocked on my door and came into my room. I felt as if I were sinking to the bottom of a featherbed as Yamileth knelt by my bedside. She held my hand and cried. A terror-stricken Miguel stood at the end of the bed, a wordless little head watching me from a distant footboard. Yamileth worried about me and what they would do without me. They were new in this country, and they needed me. Now it was my turn to say that everything would be all right, and I tried to tell them that.

When Yamileth and Miguel left our house three days later, they taped a small blue and white heart-shaped note to our bedroom door. It is still there, all these years later. It reads:

Para la Familia Hart,
Nada importa la distancia si el recuerdo de nuestra amistad
se encuentra unidad hoy y siempre.
Con cariño,
Yamileth y Miguel

(For the Hart Family,
Distance does not matter if the memory of our friendship
is united today and forever.
With affection,
Yamileth and Miguel)

Ken came, as promised, and took them to Penny and Mark's home in Lake Oswego, one of Portland's nicer suburbs.

I had the surgery; the lymph nodes were negative, but I still had six months of chemotherapy ahead of me. I learned to meditate my way through the weekly injections. I lost my hair and cultivated what I thought was an expensive "gypsy look" by wearing head scarves and hoop earrings. My body struggled, and so did my spirit.

Meanwhile, Yamileth and Miguel settled into their new life. Penny and Mark were like many people in the United States during that period in that they wanted to help Nicaraguans. Yamileth was perfect for the work in their home, and Miguel fit in with the children of the house. It was, however, Yamileth's first time away from her family for any length of time, in a completely new culture at a point when she felt particularly vulnerable and alone. In addition, the perils of being in the United States illegally were just beginning to become apparent to her.

"Penny and Mark knew I was a Nicaraguan without papers. I told them that if they still wanted to hire me, I'd do the best job possible in whatever they told me to do. I took the job because I had to work, but I was afraid, more afraid of the language than the job. What I didn't know, I'd learn, but the language? It was the first time that we were going to have contact with people who spoke only English. Mark spoke just a little Spanish and really tried hard to communicate with us, but, as it turned out, language wasn't really a problem. From what I could understand, we were the first Nicaraguans with whom they had talked. They wanted to know more about our country. It was nice that they felt moved in our presence.

"They showed me the house, and, with a lot of patience, how to work the washer and dryer. They showed me the room where we'd sleep. It was the first place I've worked where I've had my own room and my own bathroom, and carpeting everywhere. I decided that I'd definitely like working here!

"The first day, I had to learn everything. I was afraid of using the dishwasher, so for two days, I washed everything by hand. I didn't make much food because I didn't know what to cook. I told them to explain everything to me so that I could get things ready for them. In my country, we don't make large fancy meals—we weren't able to buy much—so, more than anything, I knew how to make beans, rice, and maybe some meat. Little by little they understood me and taught me.

"The first few days were the hardest because Penny and Mark went on vacation in Mexico and left us alone. We had been there so little time and I didn't know if robbers might try to break in. I felt responsible for everything. I said to myself, 'If someone breaks in to steal things, maybe the police won't believe me and instead they might think we're the robbers and that we sold everything for money.' So many things were in my head.

"We had to be ready for anything. When a tree branch broke outside, we got tense. We didn't know who could be after us. Door-to-door salesmen scared me, so we wouldn't go to the door. We were also afraid of getting lost. We had only walked a couple of blocks from the house before the family left for Mexico. There was a little plaza, as they say in Lake Oswego, where we bought sweets and little things to eat when we watched television in our room. We spent our time eating popcorn in front of the TV, and the next day we cleaned the house and ate popcorn again. That's how we lived, closed up in our room. They had given us a nice TV set to watch, so we left only to check the doors and the mail. Then we closed ourselves in the room again.

"Penny and Mark returned from their vacation and things became easier. I was still afraid to cross the streets because they had told me you could get a ticket for doing that. We Latinos aren't used to having the law enforced. In the United States, if there's a law, you have to respect it. I'm not afraid of the ticket, but I am afraid of their discovering that I'm walking around without papers. I'm always afraid the authorities will catch me.

"As time went on, I worried less because Penny and Mark always told me not to worry. If I had trouble, they'd said they'd assume financial responsibility, arrange my papers, and do whatever I wanted. But that really would have made me feel obligated to them since I often got the urge to return to my country. To have them do all that work—spending money and time arranging my papers—and then announce at the end of the week that I was leaving? So I didn't ever tell them that I'd stay. I had come with the idea of working and then returning. Be it good or bad, that was my idea.

"We all got along well and became fond of each other. I learned how to use the microwave and the vacuum. The house was small, so by noon I'd have the housework done, the clothes washed and folded, and then we worked in the yard. After Penny and Mark saw what we were doing, they bought roses and other plants. We made the yard beautiful. I never stopped working in the garden. We planted carrots, onions, lettuce. So pretty!

"While I was using an ax once, I hurt my back and it ached for days. They knew I didn't feel good, but I didn't tell them why. It embarrassed me to have hurt myself when I knew how to use an ax and hadn't gotten much work done—we like to work hard in Nicaragua—and I thought I'd get myself fired.

"I had no problems living with Penny and Mark. I told Penny to tell me when she didn't like something, and when I saw something I didn't like, I'd tell her. When it was necessary, the three of us—Mark, Penny, and I—would sit at the table and clear things up. It was a good life. They loved me a lot.

"What I've never understood, though, is that each person lives in his house but doesn't pay attention to anyone else, not even a neighbor. I don't know if it's that the other person's life has no importance or what. Here, if someone dies, so what? It's not us. We, on the other hand, are used to helping people. If someone on our block in Estelí dies, we ask if we can help. Sometimes we make coffee or spend a night in the house with the dead person. What I see here is each person for himself.

"Miguel and I slept on a small mattress on the floor because the hideabed made my kidneys hurt. One day, Penny found out and asked us why we slept there. We told her the hideabed was soft and said we slept on the floor one day and on the bed the next. But that wasn't true. Sometimes we messed up the bed just so she'd think we slept there, but we didn't. We always slept on the floor. Once she realized that, she went out and bought two beds, along with luxurious bedspreads. We had a closet for our clothes, several dressers, a television set, and a VCR, just like high-class people.

"After Penny changed the room, Miguel came in as I lay there reading with my feet crossed. 'Well, well, well, look at us!' Miguel said. 'We should have a photograph taken! If they could only see us now in Nicaragua!' We made jokes, and he teased me by saying, '*Señora*, turn on the television set, please.' The next morning I got up early to make breakfast. It wasn't my job to do that, but I thought it would help. That's how I paid back the wonderful way they treated us.

"When they came home after work, I went to my room. In general, I like to be alone. I like my privacy. I like to listen to music and watch television. I like to talk with people, but I'm not a lover of being with a crowd. I say only what's necessary.

"They liked to take us with them when they went out. Even though Penny and Mark don't have a lot of money, they belonged to a club where Miguel could swim. I didn't like to do that, though, so on my day off, Sunday, I stayed in my room and read. I hardly left the room. It embarrassed me to eat on Sunday because I felt I hadn't done anything. How could I eat if I hadn't worked? We bought tortilla chips and sodas for the room, and a creamy cheese to spread on bread, so I didn't have to leave the room to eat. I did this every week. I got some books from a library and you gave me some by Rubén Dario and Gabriel García Márquez—all too difficult with too many pages—and I'd spend the whole day reading. I didn't leave my room, I really didn't. They'd knock on the door and call, 'Yamileth, don't you want to eat?' 'No thank you,' I'd tell them. I wouldn't leave until the next day, when they'd ask me, 'Did you read the whole book?' I really liked being in that house. They loved my son, and they loved me, too.

"Miguel's shy in front of everyone, too shy even to say he's hungry. Rather than eat, he prefers to say he's not hungry. Eating embarrasses him. If he's asked if he wants something, he'll say no when he really wants it. I don't know why he's like that. He's more comfortable with adults than with children and more confident with men, no matter where we go, and will talk more with them. He talked more easily with Tomás than with you, and in Lake Oswego he talked to Mark. On Mark's day off, when he had something to do, like splitting wood, Miguel went with him. 'Mark, can I help you? You're going to the store? I'll go with you! Mark, can I wash the car for you?'

"Mark found out about a baseball team that needed more players and that would take Miguel. The team had their problems, their weaknesses, and, as they explained through Mark, no one spoke Spanish. Miguel was afraid. How would he understand? Mark patiently taught him what all the words meant, like "out" and "run," many of which were similar to Spanish. The rules in this league were different, too, from those in Nicaragua. Miguel loved it. He learned. He did everything he could.

"The team hadn't won for a long time, and after winning a game against a bigger and more experienced team, the coach announced that the only reason they had won was thanks to Miguel's energy and ability as a batter and pitcher. This wouldn't have been possible without the help of Mark. He went to all the practices with Miguel and translated for him. He devoted his day off to Miguel. I don't know how to ever pay that back. The team gave Miguel a trophy, some gloves, and a bat that go with him everywhere and that he treats like heirlooms. The coach thanked him for being the soul and nerve of the team.

"I celebrated the tenth anniversary of the triumph of the Nicaraguan Revolution, July 19, 1989, in Portland with Ken, and it made me sad. Not many Nicaraguans were there, but lots of North Americans and especially Mexicans. I saw a Nicaraguan flag and heard Nicaraguan songs. At that moment, I thought I'd never return to Nicaragua, I'd never again hear those songs there. I felt alone, and I started to feel a desperate need to be with my people."

Yamileth began to get restless. She said that she missed her people, her family. Penny and Mark even explored the possibility of bringing Leticia to Oregon. We all tried to pinpoint the problem, with the hope of being able to help. Penny brought Yamileth to Corvallis to talk with me. I learned that she did not want Leticia in Oregon, but she could not explain it further. I doubt that she knew the roots of her restlessness, and we, in her silence, were left to wonder.

After four months in Lake Oswego, Yamileth decided to return to Los Angeles. She knew she was giving up a good school for Miguel (he was thirteen and doing well in the fifth grade), a job in which she had managed to save some money, and the support of a caring family, but nonetheless she was determined to leave.

They visited us on their way south, and we took them on a three-day vacation to Black Butte Ranch, a resort in central Oregon, for their first vacation ever. Whenever I felt well enough, we walked on the paths and laughed as we sat by the pool. In nearby Sisters, we ate a *gringo* version of Mexican food, which, as usual, did not pass her taste test. She and Miguel rode bikes and took English lessons from Tom.

One evening we drove around the ranch and past homes that she again called *mansiones*. I asked Yamileth what she thought when she saw that some people had so much when others had so little. She said that those people had dreamed of building a house like that, and they had worked hard to achieve it. She, too, had a dream— that of owning a VCR; and she worked hard and was able to buy a used one. So, no, it did not bother her; she understood it. (Lisa, our daughter, upon hearing that, said, "Oh, my God, a Republican Sandinista!")

Yamileth had hopes for Los Angeles. Leticia had a job for her with a higher salary, which would allow her to return sooner to Nicaragua. In addition, Leticia's husband had thrown a vase at a new television set, shattering the screen and injuring Leticia's hand in the ensuing fight. Maybe Yamileth could help the family situation. She said that she missed her people, and we all assumed that that meant Leticia and her four daughters.

After all of our discussions, none of us was still quite sure why she was leaving. We told her that she was making a mistake. Nonetheless, in late July, she and Miguel said good-bye and took the bus to Los Angeles.

Five

The Los Angeles Battleground

—Battles follow me.

"By the time Miguel and I returned to Los Angeles, Leticia and the girls had been living in their apartment on Bonnie Brae Avenue, south of Olympic Boulevard, for several months. It's better and larger than the first one. There are two couches, both given to us by friends, and two small tables, one that came with the apartment and one that was given to us. There's one big bed, a small cot, and two mattresses. The kitchen is in the hall and is in bad shape, but the refrigerator is in the worst condition of all. There's a gas stove and a place to wash dishes. The carpeting is bad. Lots of cockroaches, rats, and mice. Miguel and I sleep on the floor, but they haven't bitten us. I've seen the rats, though, and when I get up for water at night, I see mice running around when I turn on the kitchen light.

"I made the biggest mistake of my life when I left Oregon and came back here to Los Angeles. I believed that what Leticia told me was true, even though I know Leticia lies sometimes. I made the mistake of believing that she really had work for me. My head filled up with lies. What Leticia really wanted was for me to clean the house, like a maid, and to watch over her children. 'What am I going to do in Los Angeles?' I asked her when I realized the truth. It was my biggest mistake. I've regretted leaving Oregon a thousand times.

"When I talked of wanting to be near my family, I didn't mean the family in Los Angeles. They're my family but not *número uno*. I didn't return just because they had problems. I don't get involved in marital problems, and the ones Leticia has with Sergio would have happened in Los Angeles or Estelí. I didn't miss Leticia, but I

47

did miss Omar in Nicaragua. And mostly I missed the memories of my mother.

"Leticia told me I'd make two hundred dollars a week in Los Angeles, and I'd soon have enough money to go to Nicaragua. I was desperate to return as soon as possible. I spent some of what I'd saved in Oregon to come to Los Angeles from Oregon, and here I waited, getting more anxious every day. Apparently, I had to wait for someone else to leave the job before I could have it! Just not knowing how things were in Nicaragua increased my panic. Just since I've been back in Los Angeles, people I know in Nicaragua have died, and Omar was put in prison for being absent from the military without leave. Time passed, and I made no money. The job didn't materialize, either.

"If I had stayed in Oregon, Miguel would have received a better education, learned English, and continued to advance. I wouldn't have the fear of gangs that I now have, and I'd have saved more money. I would have been able to send money to Nicaragua all along. I sent money home three times from Oregon; but from Los Angeles, only once the whole time.

"Miguel said, 'It'd embarrass me to go back to Penny and Mark after Leticia lied to you about the work you were going to have.' He said we'd return defeated and in shame. He made me feel embarrassed about having been deceived by my own family, to have left something so good and to have come here for something so bad. I couldn't bear to show my face to Penny.

"And when I realized that there was no job waiting for me in Los Angeles, I felt so alone, as if they were playing games with me. This was no laughing matter, not a game, not a joke. I don't play games with anybody, and I don't expect anyone to do so with me.

"Penny called and asked if I wanted to go back to Oregon, and I said I would return. I talked with Miguel one night while we were sleeping on the floor. I asked him what he thought, and he said, 'You said we were coming to Los Angeles to work and make more money, but we're doing nothing here. Instead, we have more problems than ever.' I started to cry. I didn't want to return to Oregon because I didn't want to see them after I had dropped everything to find a better job—after everything there had been so good—and found no job at all. Things like that can't be forgiven.

"I'd cry at night because I didn't have enough courage to tell Miguel, 'Let's go to Oregon, little one. Let's go.' I felt like the most disillusioned woman in the world. I wanted *la migra* to catch me, along with my son, and send me back to my country. Even Miguel, who doesn't think of consequences and lives only for the moment, said, 'Let's go to the places where *la migra* catches people and let them find us. That way we could go back and not pay. We'd have nothing, no clothes, but we'd be in Nicaragua.'

"If I weren't going to Nicaragua—which I plan to do in early December, this year, 1989—I'd ask Penny to forgive me. I don't know how I'd do it, but I'd go back to their family. They're good, very affectionate. I had no problems with them, and they had none with me. And I'd have Miguel go to school.**"**

Yamileth called me from Los Angeles, sounding terrified, and I had to ask her not to speak so quickly. Much as she tried to slow down, the words clipped along. A man from Sandinista State Security had just left her house. He knew that she had been in Oregon. She was not sure of the purpose of his visit; nonetheless, she asked me to obtain letters from any professors at Oregon State University and Lewis & Clark College or from solidarity groups in Corvallis and Portland with whom she had talked. The letters were to be sent directly to AMNLAE, testifying that she was helping the Nicaraguan government while she was in the United States. In Nicaragua, Yamileth had received her *militancia* from the Sandinistas, an honor awarded to a small number of people, and the letters might allow her to keep that *militancia* and protect her from whatever State Security might have in mind. A few months later, as I interviewed her, I reminded her of that fear as I listened to her calmly retell the story.

"It's true. I was afraid at first. In my country many people within the Sandinista government have emigrated after embezzling funds or robbing a place, so at that moment I was afraid. I really didn't know if he was telling me the truth, if he was returning to Nicaragua or staying here, if he had rejected the Sandinistas or the Revolution, or if he had come here to start over. If I had told him what I thought, I didn't know what his reaction would have been or whom he would have told. Maybe he came to start a pro-Contra group here, what did I know? In this life we know nothing more than the moment. When I get back to Nicaragua, I'll find out how he knew about me, of that I'm sure.

"I know him only by the name Gustavo. He's important in the Estelí government. He's a lawyer, originally from Managua, who helps people who have no money. He's not in the military. He wears civilian clothes. I think what he does here is visit members of the Sandinista party to see how things are, how we can be helped, what we've done, or to see if we're planning on staying or returning.

"The day he came to see me, he rang the bell and then knocked. I answered the door in shorts. 'Aha!' he said, 'How are you?'

" 'Fine, and you? Come in.'

"Then, as he saw that I was alone, he said, 'I'm here on the part of the Sandinista Front.'

" 'Come in. Sit down.'

"He said, 'And how's the situation here?'

" 'So-so,' I told him, 'it's fine.'

" 'Do you plan to return?'

" 'Well,' I told him, 'it's what I've intended, but I don't know what obstacles I might have to face when I go back.'

" 'What obstacles?'

" 'I don't know, but here one is far away from the news of our country.'

" 'Aha,' he said, 'so take advantage of asking whatever you want to know because I'm here, just came yesterday.' So we talked. Then I told him I might return in December, but I didn't know the date. I said nothing about getting my brother Omar out of jail because that has to be done in Nicaragua.

"He said there'd be no problems, that if people return it's because they know they're going to stay, or they don't want to stay in the United States or whatever country they're in.

"He knew I'd worked in Oregon and had given some talks. I told him that people are more interested in the progress of our country than in the politics. They want to know what will happen to the changes we've made as time goes on.

"I don't know how he found out about Oregon or how he found me. The likely explanation is that he saw a letter in Estelí that I sent to AMNLAE. If someone stopped by to visit my friends or family in Estelí and asked them what they knew about my sister and me or how they could reach us, they'd say, 'Here's the address.' The government doesn't have spies in the United States to follow people. It's too difficult to do. They don't have the capacity or the money to follow me around. He also could have found out by talking with Irene because she talks and talks, without knowing that she tells things. I knew he knew about Oregon because he asked me, 'How was it? How did it go for you in Oregon? Did it go well?' I said it was fine, and he asked, 'Why did you leave?'

" 'Because I thought I'd find better work in Los Angeles. I'll go back to Nicaragua when I get some money together, which will be easier to do from here. I understand that it's easier to take a plane from here, those things. That's why I came.'

" 'And here you've done nothing like what you were doing in Oregon?'

" 'For example?' I asked.

" 'Talking with people about the situation of our country.' That's when I realized he knew I'd been talking with people, but he said nothing more.

" 'No,' I told him, 'here I haven't had any opportunities to talk.'

" 'You haven't found a place to talk here? Or is it that you don't have the people to help you approach anyone?'

" 'Here I wouldn't know where to talk, and I don't know what problems I could encounter.' The reason I asked people to write letters about what I did in Oregon was that the letters will support me in matters that might come up when I return to Nicaragua. They'll be a backup in case something happens or when I talk with people to see if I can get Omar out of jail.

"I still wonder if he came to find out if I had remained conscientious and firm in my ideas. It was a way to get at the truth, to see if I still believe in the Revolution. I never told anyone I was going to stay here. I always said the opposite. I never said I couldn't put up with life in Nicaragua because that would've been a lie. He could have been here to attend a meeting. For example, Violeta Chamorro [who would be elected president of Nicaragua in February 1990] attends meetings in Miami, and other Nicaraguans speak to solidarity groups in Portland.

"I didn't tell anyone except you that he came. Those are my things, and I don't talk about them. My sister knows someone visited, but she also knows I don't like to talk about it. So she doesn't ask. I'm a little afraid because I'm Nicaraguan. Maybe it's because I've always been in the leadership of some organization, or that I was committed to the Revolution, to the Sandinistas. Maybe it's because we don't know the people we deal with, whether they're for the Revolution or against it. So I don't talk about politics. If anyone asks me, I know nothing.

"The Contras have people working here to convince others to finance them. Everywhere I go, I'm still afraid of the Contras. Many other Nicaraguans take advantage of the political conflict to say they're political refugees. I don't know what benefits they get, but it's easier for them because they get a permit and help from the authorities.

"I wouldn't be able to lie, to say that the Sandinistas were pursuing me. The truth is that I'm fleeing the economic situation and intend to return to my country. No way are we political refugees. In Nicaragua, if you don't like the Sandinistas, you can join another party or invent your own. More than anything, now that I'm going, I'm no longer afraid. I told him that I was trying to go in December if I got the money. It's December now and I'm leaving. If he stays here, he won't find me because I'll be gone."

In the past, when I interviewed Yamileth in her small home in Nicaragua, chickens and children provided the background noise. Family members or vegetable vendors occasionally interrupted us, military trucks roared by a few feet from the open door, and noisy Sandinista helicopters flew overhead. The country was at war, but rarely did the sounds of that war affect our conversations.

December 1989 was different. The tape recorder and the routine were the same, but the background had changed. We were in Los Angeles, and I was interviewing her at my hotel on Olympic Boulevard, just west of the Harbor Freeway. The hotel looked south to the Pico-Union area where Yamileth and thousands of other Central Americans lived, and beyond that to South-Central Los Angeles.

Los Angeles had its own war just outside the hotel and in the surrounding streets. The police attacked the gangs and the drug dealers with military-like cunning, with both the gangs and the police taking control of one area while giving up another. This war's proximity forced us, for the first time in all our years of interviewing, to close the windows and the balcony door. The police helicopters above us were so much louder, closer, and more numerous than the Sandinista helicopters had been in Estelí that Yamileth and I were unable to hear each other. Yamileth said that she had left one battle in Nicaragua only to find another one here. "Battles follow me," she said, "but I want nothing to do with them."

This new battlefield was far from the Contra war against Nicaragua, a war that we both understood, albeit differently, and a war that we both knew how to survive, she obviously more than I. But now we were in Los Angeles, where neither one of us knew the rules. Years ago, in the 1960s, I had taught ninth-grade English in the Watts area. I was there before, during, and after the Watts Riots of 1965, so inner-city Los Angeles itself was not a shock to me; nonetheless, the late-1980s version of it was.

Outside the hotel, traffic zoomed along Olympic Boulevard's broad lanes, making it initially indistinguishable from how it looked twenty-five years ago. On closer inspection, however, I noticed that security guards watched over businesses on Olympic day and night, protecting them and their employees from panhandlers, gangs, drug addicts and dealers, and thieves. The guards made up a small army available at a moment's notice. Yamileth earlier had been robbed on one of Olympic's corners. Strategically placed sawhorses stood in the middle of the side streets, and official black-and-yellow signs nailed to the sawhorses barricaded the once lovely avenues from entrance. The streets were part of a "narcotics-enforcement area," and only residents were allowed access. Helicopters hovered above, police cars patrolled the streets, and gangs sold drugs openly from their corner stakeouts. The barricades stretched south to Pico Boulevard.[1]

Yamileth and I walked to her apartment on Bonnie Brae Avenue, past the sawhorse barricades and rows of palm trees that lined the streets. Years ago, owners of the large old houses, some of which had stained-glass windows and wrought-iron grating, had divided them into high-ceilinged apartments; most now had hallway kitchens, betraying their palatial past and displaying an unsettling, modest present. Yamileth wondered where the former owners had gone and why they had left.

She and Leticia, along with their children, lived across the street from a burned-down crack house, its empty shell a warning to the neighborhood and a refuge to the homeless. Their apartment building was like all of the others on the street. The imposing front entrance opened on bleak closed doors, each one leading to separate quarters.

The family, who had never heard of gangs before they moved to Los Angeles, told me that the barricades had gone up two months ago even though dealers and gang members lived within the area. The barricades slowed down the fast-moving drug transactions.

---

[1]The irony of the use of the word "barricades" was not lost on the Nicaraguans. During the struggle to overthrow Somoza, they pulled up the paving stones in the streets to make barricades. Miguel's father had been killed by a paving stone that hit him in the chest during one of the final battles in 1979. A pro-Sandinista newspaper in Managua is called *Barricada*.

Latinos sold the drugs on the street, coming by foot and occupying every corner. Since the buyers came in cars, the barricades mostly affected them, but they also alerted sellers and potential buyers that police and helicopter surveillance had intensified.

Like a nervous beast, night settled heavily and warily over South-Central Los Angeles, as it did every night. Most Central Americans stayed home, as did Yamileth and her family, afraid to venture out.

"In order to avoid problems, we almost never use the main door. We avoid communication with others in the building because we don't know what kind of people they are. All I know is that the owner is a Nicaraguan woman, and her brother lives in one of the apartments. Many of the renters in the building are involved in drugs, so we don't get involved in their problems or allow them to get involved in ours. I never open the front door, never, and we leave only through the back.

"Twice, thieves stole guns, money, television sets, VCRs from a woman upstairs. She accused me of stealing her things and said the police were coming to check the house. I know that in this country I could have sued her for saying things that aren't true. I consulted a lawyer, and Leticia told the woman we were filing a complaint, but I decided against it. Things are different from our country. Legally, here it's necessary to be careful when saying anything to anyone. Some Latinos have already learned *el tejemaneje*, the dirty tricks, and take advantage of the situation in order to get money. The gangs are called *pandillas*, *cholos*, or *bandas*. In this area they're all Latinos, but they communicate in English. They've been in the United States a long time. You can tell that by the way they dress, move, walk, the way they cut and comb their hair.

"The other night around eight o'clock, I had to go to the liquor store for Alka-Seltzer, and the gangs were on the corner, talking in English. They hid a letter behind a wall, and I saw them do it. You can't let these people know you've seen anything because they think you'll turn them in. Then they'll beat you, even beat you to death, so you go along pretending you don't see anything. But I saw them hide the letter. They must have taken it from someone, but I've no idea who. When the gangs sell drugs, they make signs and gestures with their hands and display a small white package with cocaine in it, the only drug I've heard of on the street. If you want to leave this area at night, you have to drive quickly. Otherwise, they damage the car by throwing rocks.

"In Nicaragua we know who our enemies are. I can spot them by how they're dressed, by the guns they carry. I know if I walk at the head of a battalion, people in the countryside will help me locate the enemy or tell me where they went. Then we either follow them or wait for them. I even know what weapons they have.

"The enemy in Pico-Union is different from the enemy in Nicaragua. It's hard for me to tell what kind of person I'm meeting up with, what kind of evildoer—a rapist, a murderer—will confront me. Here they're in groups, in gangs, wearing civilian clothes and hiding short steel knives and firearms. I get frightened when I see four or five youths on the corner. Maybe they're planning to rob me or waiting to kill someone.

"If I'm in Estelí, it's unlikely that I'll meet up with an armed Contra walking peacefully down the street. I might meet people who work with the Contras—disguised and doing other work—but it'd be difficult for them to walk around with a gun killing people. But here, people do it. They damage police vehicles, break car windows, and attack the police themselves. They're dangerous young men. They don't respect anyone who tries to stop them. Gangs divide the territory up. They say, 'This is my territory, and that's yours.' If a gang gets involved in another's territory, they quarrel among themselves. Defenseless people come down the street, maybe to buy food for their families, and are assaulted or killed, leaving the rest of the family without money and their daily food.

"The authorities haven't found out how to rehabilitate the ones they arrest. They've been too easy on them. It's of no use to arrest them and then have the families take them home right away. A child just returns to his gang. The game goes on.

"If the police do show up, the gangs are gone. It's an accident if the police catch them. The police go over there, and the gang comes here. Every day there are more well-armed little groups directed by someone destroying young people. Stopping all this is like taking a whisker off a cat [and getting scratched in the process].

"Sometimes the police close off several blocks around where we live, and the patrols step up. They focus their lights on houses, and helicopters often fly over with infrared lights. The police effort is so big that the other day, around noon, one helicopter and seven patrol cars chased just two men. When the police close off our area, they allow no one to enter except those who live here. If you come in a vehicle, they let you park it, but if you—man or woman—come on foot, they stop you. If you have documents, they let you go, but if you have none, they send you to jail and investigate you. For all these reasons, we avoid going out.

"I've heard shots at night, close by. Since Miguel and I sleep on the floor next to the window, it frightens us because I know stray bullets can hurt people. I had often heard shots at night in Nicaragua, but it was different because I knew the reasons, the problems, and where they might occur. And I knew what I should do, depending on the country's situation and state of alert. But in the United States I don't know where the shots are going to come from, or why, nor do I know what I should do. I hear shots outside, but I can't leave. It'd be like putting myself in the wolf's mouth. There's more tension in Los Angeles, more than in the war in Nicaragua. That's why I would prefer to be in my country."

To the north of her apartment and my hotel, up busy Alvarado Street that served as the shopping center for the area, lay MacArthur Park, immortalized years ago in a song written by Jimmy Webb and sung by Richard Harris. When I moved to Los Angeles in the early 1960s, the elegant park and the nearby Bullock's Wilshire department store reminded me of F. Scott Fitzgerald's Los Angeles of the 1940s and 1950s. I bought my wedding dress at Bullock's; and, over the years, the park became one of my favorite places in the city.

By the time Yamileth arrived in Los Angeles, police entered the park only in protective numbers. Immigration officers often swept the park and pulled everyone into their net, handcuffing them before putting them in a van and deporting them. Prudent Latin Americans such as Yamileth walked on the other side of the street from the park, not through it. People bought and used drugs there, and the homeless slept under palm trees. People were murdered, and some were born. The park that I remembered was gone well before the city dug it up, made it a metro stop, and then rebuilt the lake.

"I get nervous when I go near MacArthur Park. I'm afraid the authorities will catch me and send me out of the country without my being able to say good-bye. It'd be all right if *la migra* caught me with Miguel, but the possibility of being caught alone worries me so. I couldn't protest because I don't have the right. I'd have to leave without saying anything or asking for anything, with only the hope that they'd send Miguel to Nicaragua. That's what scares me.

"I usually don't walk to MacArthur Park. I've gone to that area by car with Leticia. We get out of the car, buy what we have to buy, and leave. I don't like to go with another Latino. If something terrible happened, that person probably wouldn't know what to do, either. Most are undocumented. What could we do if we were picked up? It's better to be on a street with all kinds of people and not be on a street with just Latinos, especially not one full of police or drug dealers. Often, gangs and lots of Latinos are involved in drugs. I like to walk down a peaceful street where there are no gangs, only people leaving for work and returning. And lots of different kinds of people.

"*La migra* comes to the park almost daily but especially on weekends along with the police. Patrols circle the park, then go in and round up everyone. I've seen that happen twice, from cars, and it scares me. Simply out of fear, I go no closer than across the street.

"Even so, I think *la migra* will see me watching and deport me. They have enough experience to know just by seeing me. They don't see it in the way we dress, but they do in our faces or the way we walk. Lots of Latinos get nervous, just as I do, and *la migra* spots that fear. They know if you have papers or not. We run because we're scared, and either the police or *la migra* comes after us. They don't know if we're running because we're illegal or because we have drugs, but they find out.

"While you and I were walking toward the park, I heard Latinos offering drugs to the person behind us. They also openly offered him a false immigration permit and a false Social Security number. They said, 'False papers?' to me, too. I could ask how much they'd charge me for a phony Social Security number, and they'd make it for me quickly. All they need is my name, and five or ten minutes later I'd have it.

"I don't know which people are *la migra*. I don't know who, of the people dressed in military clothes, has the right to kick someone out. I'll leave this country still not knowing who's who. So I'm afraid of going out, of even going to a restaurant, especially in Los Angeles. Many times, people have been caught in Latino restaurants and coffee shops. Whenever I go to a restaurant, I'm afraid that will happen to me. I know I'll be leaving, but I don't want them to throw me out."

Leticia and Sergio soon separated. Moving to the United States had not solved the problems they had had in Nicaragua. He lived with his mother, gave Leticia no money, and on occasion took Nora somewhere, but no one else. Would he have behaved like that if he were still in Nicaragua? Had the United States changed him? It is hard to say. I talked with a Los Angeles bank security guard, a Latino, who told me that the Latinos in the neighborhood did not take care of their children. Yamileth agreed and disagreed.

"Latinos generally take care of their families, but when they come to the United States, their customs are forced to change. They change because of their work. The more hours you work, the more you earn. People have to have two jobs, which leaves no time to take care of children.

I worry that if I devote myself to work, I won't be close to the children. I won't even know where they are. According to statistics from Nora and Miguel's school, most parents don't go to school meetings, and the school says that having to work isn't a justification to miss meetings. Sometimes teachers don't realize what sacrifices parents make to support their children. They don't know if the head of the family is a single woman who'd have to leave work to go to the meeting, or if the day of the meeting isn't her free day, or if her children's food depends on her work. For Latinos, there must be a way to find an alternative to those meetings.

"At the same time, Latin American families are overprotective. We're obsessed with our children. We find it hard to understand that our children, when they become adults, need to make their own decisions. It's difficult because we're so attached, so full of love, so protective. It's too much, and that's bad, especially if there's no father.

"Even though I know better, I made the same mistake with my son. We, mothers and fathers alike, consider ourselves lord and master of the child. No one else has any authority over him. My mistake was keeping my son close to me, and I recognize it. I shouldn't be like that, but I can't stop it.

"We haven't all lived the same life. For example, neither Omar nor I had a childhood. We didn't do things like go to the park to have fun. We worked just to survive; and then, later, we struggled to overthrow Somoza. We gave our youth to the Revolution. As a result, we're always worried that the same thing might happen to our children, and we won't let that happen. Our past has influenced how we see our own children.

"At the same time, a person who hasn't had a childhood finds it difficult to understand a child. When Miguel, now thirteen, plays with cars or plays hide-and-seek, it disgusts me sometimes. I force myself to play with him and not to scold him. Sometimes, Omar forces himself to make little toys for his children, but neither one of us likes to see children play, especially when they're so big. Omar and I never did those things, and that's why we called ourselves *pobrecitos*, poor little things.

"I've heard Omar call the children lazy, using a vulgar Nicaraguan word: 'You've become *huevones*[2]; now it's time to get to work. You're grown up now. You're men. You should be working, not playing with little cars!' He's said that, and so have I. I've said to Miguel, 'My little love, you should be looking for work, even if it's washing cars. You'd have money instead of asking me all the time.' He just looks at me as if he's trying to understand me, and that bothers me. So I try to find a way to get back in his good graces. I just never want him to put up with what I had to. Certainly, I want him to study, because you can get along better in life if you're not illiterate. Many of us have had hard lives, and not all of us have been lucky, so we'll continue to make the mistake of being tied to the family and protecting them from the things we lived through.

"I like it when Miguel talks with Tomás, with Ken, with Mark. They transmit how to be a man to him since I don't have one to help me with this. In Nicaragua, Omar would say, 'Look, Miguel, men have to do this and that. They have to work. Your mama can't be with you all the time.' Sometimes, Miguel doesn't think. If I have a television set that breaks down, he thinks that someday someone will fix it, but he personally doesn't worry about it. I could give it to him and say, 'This is yours, and you must take care of it,' but I don't do that.

"In Nicaragua we always have our family near, ready to help each other, to get together when we can. Some marry and still live in the same house with their parents. That's not good. It's better if children get married and have their own family somewhere else. That way, they take care of themselves and don't end up being the responsibility of their parents. On the other hand, children have too much freedom in the United States. I don't think that families made that decision, but that's what's happened.

"We're more bound to each other financially, it seems. Certainly, it's true in my feelings of responsibility toward Omar, but Leticia doesn't feel the same way. All the time I've been here, she hasn't sent any money to Nicaragua, except the one time she sent

---

[2]*Huevones* can be translated as "lazy bastards." *Huevo* in Spanish means egg; in slang, it means testicle. The inference is that a man's testicles are so big that they encumber his movements, thus making him lazy.

fifty dollars to an aunt for an operation. I don't think I made a defi-
nite promise about money to Omar, but it bothers me because I
have food. Maybe I make only enough for that, but I eat. Since
Omar's in prison, he's without work, without a salary, with only
his family and a sick infant. Since I know what it's like to have
nothing to eat, I'm concerned about him. I always have been.

"Even though Omar and I are children of the same mother, we
haven't had the same opportunities. The chances I had through the
revolutionary process have been different from his; but, at the same
time, he rejected many opportunities, mainly because he's been so
tied to his wife, Irene. Or maybe out of affection for my mother.
I'm not the one to say, only he. But what he did was to turn down
chances in the Sandinista military to be better educated, to leave
the country on a scholarship for technical training. One offer for
one year, another for two years, and one for more time than that.
Irene would even have received money while he was out of the
country. If it had been me, I would have gone wherever they sent
me, just to see what happened. In the military, if they had decided
to send me somewhere thinking that I'd like it, I'd like it. But he
didn't like the idea of studying and leaving Nicaragua. He'd have
earned more money afterward, but he wouldn't even go to a year-
long course in Managua. In Managua! He could have returned to
Estelí on the weekends or every month. But he didn't go. The fault
is really his.

"From what neighbors and relatives have written me, Omar's
problems started when we left. Alone, with no support, and probably disenchanted, he went drinking for two weeks without having
gotten permission from the military. During those two weeks of
drinking, he didn't come home some nights. Maybe he'd show up
the following day, but he was always drinking. He slept, then left,
and lost himself again. I suppose he did it until he got tired, maybe
eight or ten days of it, and then he tried to sleep it off and recover.
Afterward, when he realized what he had done, he hid in the house.
When he showed up at work, they took him prisoner.

"The neighbors said he cried when he drank. He said his sisters
had thrown him out, he had no mother, no sisters, nothing, and
what was he going to do without a family? He has always had his
weaknesses but has never before missed work. I think our mother's
death and our leaving left him feeling so abandoned that nothing,
not even his own children, mattered to him. He thinks that since I
came here—in his mind I'm surrounded by dollars and everything

good—I'll forget him. He thinks that my coming here made him drink and be irresponsible.

"To make matters worse for me, his son wrote me a letter and said, '*Tía* Yamileth, my papa has been drinking because you left. He went to clean my grandmother's grave, and he cried. Why did you leave him?'

"When you do what Omar did, you feel morally destroyed. Your children say things like, 'Papa, why are you doing that? Why are you drinking?' Omar, though, said he learned from the experience. He wrote, 'I feel alone. Now that I'm in prison, none of my drinking buddies has come by. I'm sick, and they don't come to see me. The only ones who have come have been my children and my wife.'

"Family unity comes and goes, and much of it left with the death of my mother. Omar made her dance on the thirtieth of May, the Mother's Day before she died, and we had a little party. At that moment the family was united, close, and understanding in the midst of all the things we lacked. Perhaps we shared all these things because we loved our mother. She was the center. In order to share with her, we had to get together in that center, her house. We made dinner, and my brother got her to dance. And she was sick! Even though she felt worse after dancing, she was happy to share that with her children.

"Our mother was what united us. Through her sincerity she kept us together. She shared everything. If Leticia said, 'Mama, why don't you give me a little of that?' she'd say, 'Take it.' Then Omar would come by: 'Do you have a little soap left from what Yamileth gave you?' 'Take it.' Years ago, when Omar came home from fighting in the mountains and brought things given to him by *campesinos*—beans, hot chiles—he'd leave a little at each house. When Leticia had extra money—she has always made more than the rest of us—she gave it to my mother so that she could buy something. In that sense there was communication and unity.

"If my mother were alive, I wouldn't be in the United States. Nor would Omar be in prison, nor would he ever have left his job. More than anyone, he suffers from the family's being separated. Leticia has always been somewhat separate from the rest of us, but Omar and I were close, listening to music together and going to the river with the children. We suffered most from our mother's death and the separation from each other, which will serve to unite us when I return to Nicaragua. We'll see with more maturity the errors we've made. We'll be closer and rectify the bad things we did.

"It's harder here in Los Angeles. Once my nieces called me a terrible name, *una gran boluda*. It means you're lazy. I've never been a lazy person who wanted to be supported by someone else. Never. I've never liked anyone to give me something if I don't do anything to earn it. Leticia has said things indirectly, not right to my face, but she's said, 'It's outrageous! There are no women in this house to put things away and clean up. There are only loafers here, and they do nothing. I'm the only one who works around the house.' I clean up, but when they all come home, they mess it up again. I feel like Cinderella, just taking care of everything in the house without being able to leave to do something else. And still, they're not satisfied.

"The same day Leticia made those comments, I said, 'Look, Leticia, I'm the only person who takes care of the house, and you also know I'm the only person in this house who isn't working. You should say things directly to me if you have a problem. I do everything possible to clean up the house, but what happens is that none of your children, not you either, does anything to maintain order. When you get up in the morning, you leave this pile of clothes you throw out of the closet for someone else to put back in order. If I had charged you, you'd still owe me money.'

"The girls never clean up. When I knew you were coming, Diana, I told them not to shame themselves and to clean up the house. '*Ay, Tía,*' they said, 'we don't want to do it. You come and do it.' They think I'm a maid, that I'm obliged to do everything.

"The girls spend their lives fighting. When I hear them doing that, I just leave, go outside and down the street. It really bothers me. What's more, it embarrasses me to have the neighbors hear it and know what they're saying. The people on the other side always listen. So I go outside while the girls yell and kill each other. When I leave, I scream, 'I'm going. Let me know which one got murdered so that someone can come to take away the body.'

"When we lived together in Nicaragua, it was one big battle. Chela even tried to hit me. I struck her and pushed her away. I immediately said, 'If you want to go, go. I take no responsibility for you.' Marisa tried to step in, but I said, 'Look, Marisa, if she wants to go, let her. I'm not going to keep poorly brought-up and disobedient children in my house. Your mother told me to take care of you and protect you the best I can. I'm not making a cent by having you here. She sends me nothing.' The fact was that she sent all the money to Marisa, and Marisa shopped only for what we needed for the moment, not long range. I often had to use what little money of my own that I had because the prices rose every day, and it's better to buy food ahead of time to last you through the week or month.

"Chela told Miguel that he was a scavenger, that we ate everything, and that they were supporting him as well as me. That made me cry. I've said nothing to Leticia. I didn't want them to see me crying. And Leticia didn't ask if we had eaten. I felt so embarrassed. Worse than the gynecological exam!

"In spite of everything, I've been contributing to the food, rent, telephone. I've never failed, with the exception of November and this week in December 1989. I stopped working in the middle of November because I had this trip coming up. I'd been caring for a child, taking another to school, and selling clothes and cosmetics. I also spent time looking for work, but everywhere I went they asked for papers, for documents. I needed money, and there was nothing in the house to eat. Leticia and my nieces won't accept the idea that there's not enough money for the month, so they save nothing.

"There are seven or eight of us, and we all eat together at night. During the day, only Nora, Miguel, and I eat. The two older ones who go to school come home at four o'clock. Marisa and Leticia eat when they get home at night. And the rent is four hundred fifty dollars. The telephone is fifty, sometimes more, sometimes less. People call from Nicaragua when they're having operations or need to ask us for something. They always say it's urgent, so we always take the call.

"So that the school wouldn't charge me for the food Miguel and Nora ate, I told the principal some truth and some lies, and she gave the children food. For example, I told her that we hadn't been here long, that I didn't have work, and that we were alone. That right now I was helping a woman sell clothes but it didn't pay well, only one hundred dollars a month.

"When I was in Oregon and they were in Los Angeles, Nora didn't go to school because no one took her. Now that I'm back, I take care of her, give her something to eat, and take her to school every day. People here pay forty, fifty dollars a month to have that done. I pick her up at three o'clock, but no one takes that into account. It's not much, true, but a conscientious person would see what someone does for others. But they don't notice, nor do they ask if we've eaten or not.

"A man gave me a job cleaning his office, an old man, sick with sugar in his blood, who had lived in both Guatemala and Mexico. When I work, I work. I don't hang around and talk a lot. Still, the man was interested in me as a woman. I saw him as a good man, nothing more. He brought me home on Sundays and would say, 'Do you and your son want to go out?' So we'd take advantage of the chance to eat and go out.

"One day he said, 'Come, let's go to the supermarket and see what we can buy for the house. Don't you want me to buy something?' It was as if he realized how little we had. I feel bad about it now, but I took advantage of him and bought lots of things that would hold us for a long time. No one in the house even asked where I had gotten everything. He bought Miguel a pair of pants, and once he said, 'Here, little one, take this twenty-dollar bill,' trying to gain Miguel's affection. We saved the twenty dollars.

"His ideas were different from mine, and I wouldn't lie to live a lie. He wanted me to live with him and tried to tempt me by saying that Miguel would live well. I'm not really interested in material things, and I didn't want to deceive him, either. I told him I was returning to Nicaragua because I had lots of problems with my family here. It would have been a real shock to Miguel if I had gone to live with a man right off the bat.

"Someone must have told him that Miguel and I slept on the floor, because one day he brought a mattress to the house for us. One night my back hurt, so I put the blanket on the floor and slept there. Leticia came in, grabbed the mattress, and she and her boyfriend Roberto slept on it. Now they have it, and we're permanently back on the floor.

"The boyfriend's Salvadoran. He says he's a *guerrillero*, but that's a lie. He's a man without shame and an opportunist. In the time I've known him, he hasn't had a job. He lives at the expense of Leticia, and that's why the money doesn't last. He always has his *cervecitas*, his little beers, and his food. If there's no food, she takes him out to eat without asking anyone else to go along.

"It bothers everyone to have Roberto around. The children are afraid to criticize their mother because Leticia doesn't accept criticism from anyone, nor does she take any abuse from anyone. Marisa, who works and helps pay the rent, doesn't like Roberto. That's why she doesn't buy food. Why buy food if that guy just eats it? The way I see it, Leticia has this man, so let her figure out how to pay for things. Leticia becomes unbearable sometimes. She flares up in a moment. Who could put up with her?

"And the boyfriend, well, he supposedly has a job lined up for tomorrow, but that's a problem because yesterday he was in jail.[3] Today, too. I don't know what he did, and Leticia hasn't said anything to me, probably because one day, in front of her, I said to him, 'You're telling me to stay in the United States. But why should I stay here? To live like you? If I want to live here, I'll live here, but you, you're a parasite!' I continued, all in front of Leticia. 'I didn't leave my country to come here to be a parasite, to let someone support me and do nothing. That's not progress. You have no shame.' The beer he was drinking and the food he was eating were bought by someone else. I said that neither he nor Leticia knew or cared how much he consumed each week and what it cost.

"Then he got angry and said, 'You've no business getting involved in our lives.'

" 'I'm not involved,' I said. 'When have I gotten into your business? The only thing I'm telling you is the truth. As far as I'm concerned, you can pack your bags. I'm not used to seeing men kept by women. It's not that way in our country. Men and women both work so that they can live together and share the needs of the house. That's what I'm used to, not to things like this.'

"I'm a little hardened, I think. Sometimes I don't like the way I am. I shouldn't be like that when I'm talking with someone. I've never shown fear to anyone, never. Maybe respect, but not fear. And I respect anyone who treats me with respect, not just because it might be an older person, but because in this life all human beings deserve respect. An example is Roberto. I didn't talk to him in an affectionate way. I'm always defensive. I get indignant, and I make myself defensive. That's a mistake on my part.

"Even with Miguel I've been rude. It must be nerves. Being nervous makes me anxious, to the point that I'm not hungry and I don't want anything to eat, not anything. When someone asks me something, I yell, 'Not now!' Then I think I should never have yelled. Miguel complains, 'Why are you yelling at me like that?' Then I calm down.

"I worry when the children go out with other people, older ones, and come home late. If they go to the beach, I worry about sharks. It's nervous tension. Life here is pure tension.**"

---

[3]According to both Leticia and Roberto, he interfered with the arrest of a young Latino on the corner of Vermont and Pico and was taken to jail. Once there, the computer showed that he had two parking tickets that he had to pay before being released. He was freed two days later. His job was in "parking."

After hearing Yamileth talk so much about Uncle Mundo, he became an unlikable character in my mind. I met him once in Managua. He had been napping; and when he walked by me, he tousled his hair and glanced curiously, looking nondescript and sleepy. Long before the trip from Nicaragua to the United States, his temper frightened Yamileth and the children. It kept them in check until Mexico City, when Yamileth and Sofía had the argument with him. That broke the fear. Well before they reached the U.S. border, Yamileth knew he was afraid. His control was over.

She heard that, after the Christmas party in Mexico, Mundo's brother-in-law warned him about her, saying that he should be careful because Yamileth was a Sandinista and might be fleeing. Yamileth laughed out loud. Mundo was the one who was in trouble with the authorities, not she. What his trouble was, she was never quite sure, but his fear was alive. She felt it starting from the time they left Guatemala, and its source wasn't worry about them. He was more afraid for himself.

When he told her months later in Los Angeles that she owed him five hundred dollars for the trip to the United States, she became rightfully angry. I asked her if she had paid Mundo.

"No, I haven't paid Mundo! He was here about a month ago. He called me on the phone and said, 'Yamileth, I'm here, in Los Angeles.'

" 'Oh, yes,' I said, 'and when did you come? I'm happy that you're here.'

" 'When are you going to pay me?'

" 'Listen, Mundo, why don't you come over here so that we can talk? I'm not going to go to your house.'

" 'Okay, I'll be there.'

" 'If Sergio's there, tell him that he can come, too. Leticia isn't here, but the children will soon be home from school.'

"So they both came, and once again Mundo asked me when I was going to pay him.

" 'Listen, Mundo and Sergio,' I said, 'you think I owe you money. Right?'

" 'Yes.'

" 'Then just when did I make that agreement with either one of you?' I was angry but tried to hide it. 'Mundo, when did you tell me that you were bringing me here and for how much money?'

" 'I didn't.'

" 'And you, Sergio, when did you tell me?'

" 'I didn't.'

" 'So! Then what is it I owe you? I don't owe you anything!'

" 'But Leticia . . .'

" 'Aha! So Leticia made the agreement? I didn't.'

"Sergio started shouting at me, 'I don't have to pay for you and Miguel!'

" 'I didn't ask for anything!' I yelled back. 'I don't know who came up with the idea that I bring your children to this country, that I take care of them so that nothing happened to them along the way. Wasn't that why you brought me here? And now, what do you want? If you want to wait, I'll call Leticia and tell her to come right away. Let's settle this once and for all, but I'm not going to pay.'

"So I called her and told her that Mundo and Sergio were here to collect money from me. I told her I wanted to know what money they were talking about because I had never made any agreement with them. 'Put them on the phone,' she said. After they had talked with her, I wanted to, also. 'Look, Leticia, I don't owe Mundo a dime, nor do I owe Sergio anything. I made no agreement to pay to bring your children here!'

"I gave the phone back to Mundo, and Leticia said, 'I don't understand, Mundo, why you and Sergio and your mother are charging Yamileth. You made the agreement with me. Besides, the amount you're charging her isn't what we agreed upon. You gave me one amount for everyone. I didn't ask you for a separate price for each one.'

"I told them to just forget their idea that I owed them anything. 'And don't call me again,' I added. 'I don't want to be bad, but I know you're a *coyote* and bring people here. I also know the address of your house in Mexico, and I have a photo of you. I can give it to the authorities here, so don't make trouble for me.' That was an absolute lie. I don't have a photo of him, but he knew me well enough to know that when I said something, I meant it. Neither one of them ever came back to ask me for anything.**"**

Besides taking care of children and cleaning offices, the only work Yamileth could find was selling cosmetics, as her nieces and her sister did. It was awkward for her since she had never paid that much attention to how she looked, preferring to dress in jeans.

"When I sold cosmetics, I always explained that I didn't use makeup, but according to the experience of my sister and others, the products were good. I couldn't say so from my own experience.

Still, people bought it. It's a well-known product, and people like it. I usually sold it in beauty salons, places where they sold makeup, perfume, fingernail polish, lipstick, blush, skin cream, pills to make you thin, pills for all sorts of things.

"I was offered a job at a place called the Institute, but the job was to go out and sell courses to Latinos. I'd receive sixty dollars for each contract I sold. For example, a nurse's course took six months and cost two hundred sixty dollars—sixty for me and two hundred for the man. It didn't matter if the person actually went or not. I couldn't figure out how I'd sell the courses if I hadn't taken them. People would certainly ask, 'Have you taken the class? Is it a good class?' The nurse's class, for example, how could I guarantee that? That people would learn to be a nurse in six months? I told the Institute no, I couldn't do it.

"I tried to find other work and had lots of interviews. They all said they'd let me know tomorrow, and they never called back. Once a woman wanted me to work at night, but she paid only thirty dollars a week. And I had to stay overnight and pay for two buses. Most of the money went to the bus. I didn't take the job.

"Really, when you see these things in the paper and just go there, well, it frightens me. Once I called about a job and found out a single man wanted his house cleaned. I was scared. I know that some people abuse those whom they hire, force them into sex, what do I know?

"I did find a job, but I don't know the name of the place, nor do I know if it really is a cantina. The woman didn't give me a name when she told me about the work. She said a restaurant needed waitresses. I needed work, so I wanted to try it. It paid well, she said. For each beer you served, you made five dollars. It must be a good place, I thought, to pay that amount for serving beer. It must be a luxurious place! So I concerned myself with what I was going to wear. Sofía lent me a dress that was too short for her but fit me. And some black shoes. She gave me some panty hose—supposedly it was an important place—and fixed my hair.

"I left with the woman and her sister at half past five in the afternoon. I know nothing about Los Angeles, so I had no idea where we were. When we arrived, I saw some men outside, the type of men I had never imagined. They were Latinos, but the kind who drink too much liquor. Their clothes were not how I imagined the clientele would dress. Neither was the place what I imagined. As I entered, I noticed that it was so dark that people could barely see each other. There was little light, and the place was small, with hardly any seats. Three women waiting at the bar were dressed in a way that shocked me, that wasn't proper for the luxurious place I had imagined. Their clothes almost showed part of their underpants and their breasts. And they had on too much makeup. It surprised me.

"The woman immediately said, 'If the men ask you to dance, dance. If a man invites you to have a beer with him, tell him you'll get it. Your beer costs the man seven dollars. When you go to the bar to buy it, give two dollars to the woman bartender, and take five dollars for yourself.' The men, even though they are Latinos, know that they can buy beer cheaper somewhere else. Men aren't going to pay seven dollars a beer just for the taste. They come to enjoy themselves with the women.

"The women didn't make enough to live on. Maybe they needed the beer, or maybe they liked that kind of crowd, or liked men hugging them. There was a musical group playing music typical of *campesinos*, country music but not mariachi, more like music of Los Tigres del Norte.[4] There also were some little girls, not very old, minors. Whenever the police come, the women hide them in the kitchen. What they're doing there isn't honest.

"I saw other women who had had too much to drink. They came, not to make money selling beer, but to be with men. They were paid to make love. I saw women leave with men and return in two or three hours. In fact, I went there with three women, and one of them disappeared with some men, and I didn't know where.

"I began to be afraid. There was almost no place for me to sit. There were no tables, so I had to stand up. I managed to take a little chair from a man and sat in a dark corner, close to the bathroom. Men tried to force me to dance. I told them no, that I didn't want to dance, that I was worn out, that I was tired. I pointed out other women to them, told them to look for someone else. Really, I didn't like it. One of them became mean, but I didn't give in. I had no energy. I wasn't ready to play the game. I sat there until half past two in the morning. I didn't know where I was or how to return, and I didn't have money for a taxi. I had no alternative other than to wait until the woman decided to take me home.

"She called for a taxi. On the way home, she asked me if I had liked it. I told her it wasn't that I didn't like it, it was that I didn't

---

[4]Los Tigres del Norte is the number one *norteño* (northern) music group in Mexico as of this writing. *Música norteña* is perhaps best compared to U.S. country music, although the analogy is not perfect.

see it as a way to make money. Then she told me, 'Don't worry. The second night will go better for you, and the third even better than the second.' I got home tired, so tired. Being in that place exhausted me.

"I was ashamed when my nieces asked me how the work went, but I told them about it so that they would be careful when they were offered work. If I had seen the danger ahead of time, I could've handled it differently.

"The following afternoon, the woman called and asked if I was getting ready. I told her I couldn't go because someone had brought me a child to take care of. That wasn't the truth, but I couldn't figure out another way to say it. She called me several times after that. I told her no, I was going to continue selling clothes and taking care of that child. I gave her lots of excuses because I didn't feel good about telling her the truth. She liked her work and even took her younger sister with her. They liked it, but I didn't. I thought the woman would have felt ashamed had I told her the truth.**"**

When I interviewed Yamileth in Los Angeles in 1989, I also visited our daughter Lisa, who had just finished college and was teaching in the area before joining the Peace Corps. Yamileth was impressed that Lisa was on her own and no longer financially dependent on us. She did not think that her nieces would ever be in the same situation and be that independent, nor would they ever have the same goals that had inspired Yamileth to work hard in Nicaragua.

"What's the future here? I've talked with many people about this. To come to the United States, have your children study, and then have them be too lazy to work? That's not my idea of the future. I don't see it, really I don't. Children learn English but spend their days strolling around, drinking, and playing. That's the future? For me the future is thinking about tomorrow and preparing yourself for it. The only heritage a parent can leave is the intellectual preparation of a child, not a chair or a house that they can sell. An education allows them to fight for survival, wherever they go. No one can take away that inheritance.

"We fight for our children to have a profession, but it's a constant battle. Children come to the United States, study, but don't take advantage of the opportunities. They do nothing. It doesn't matter to them. They leave their countries to come here, and it becomes worse. If they do get educated, they just become corrupted. What kind of future is that? Leticia spends what she makes. Where are her savings? One comes here to save so that you can start your own business or return to your country and use your money to help. But to live just to live! I don't get it. No one has been able to answer that question. None of the people I've talked with.

"And from what I can see in the Los Angeles schools, math is much further behind and taught with a different methodology. Miguel's studying things in the fifth grade that he studied in the third grade, but in a different way. The reading doesn't demand much. They just let the person read the way they were reading. In Nicaragua, he had to explain what he read so that they knew he understood. The homework isn't hard here. He just has to fill in the blanks. No one explains anything. He doesn't know what he did; neither does the teacher. They give him a good grade without knowing. And it's easy to cheat. So you don't know who's educated and who's not.

"It's not that I prefer the schools in Nicaragua. We often don't have chalk, and we have trouble with the teachers. I just wish they didn't make the work so easy here. It'd be better if they pushed the students more. I wish they wouldn't give work that's already done and they'd try to get the students more interested. I know, everything's here, teachers, materials, everything, and I'm grateful to the school for taking my son and for giving him food all this time. It'd be hard to pay for it. I don't know whom to thank. But each country has its customs. I respect the education here, but I also like it in Nicaragua, in spite of all the difficulties we have.

"And then there are the gangs. The school asked us to talk with our children. Parents have to know the colors the gangs like so that when children say to us, 'Let's buy a suit of such-and-such a color, and shoes like that,' we know. Gangs like blue and lots of gold jewelry on their arms. Even their haircut is different and the way they comb it. A loose shirt, the color black, and just the way of leaning against a car.

"That's one of the biggest reasons for my wanting to return to Nicaragua. I don't want a Saint Miguel, a holy man. I want him to know life, to be able to stand up for himself, to fight if he has to, to learn a profession, to study, to have some advantages. But not to be a gang member.

"And then there's David. From the time I left Nicaragua, I've had little or no communication with him. I don't know what the situation will be when I return, but I do know things will change. I'm not going to try to reconcile with him. I won't try to justify anything—that would be disgraceful—but I want to talk with him, be friends, and be able to see him. I also want him to see the cream-colored *guayabera* shirt I'm bringing him. Accepting gifts is a problem within the military. If I come from the United States with something sophisticated, well, it's better to come with something simple, like soap or maybe underwear.

"Communication between us is prohibited. If David had enough confidence in me to tell me military secrets, then the U.S. government or some organization could use me to get information. I can't even send a letter directly to my own brother because he's in the military, but I do it through other people. I send letters to Alejandra to find out about David. I trust her. She's been the go-between for my conversations with him, for my being able to see him, for my being able to go with him. I ask her how he is, what problems he might've had with his children, things like that. I tried to find out if he has seen his children much, if he's helped them, what he bought for them on payday. I want him to feel responsible. He's in the military and has to set an example.

"But I haven't heard. I know Alejandra got the letter, but if the situation's difficult, she might not be allowed to travel out of town. If you're out of your territory and get attacked by the Contras, the government doesn't assume any responsibility. David's still in the town near Estelí, but it's dangerous to travel in that direction. The road's bad, lots of mountains, and not many houses. After many conflicts with the Contras, the military closed the road. I suppose I'm trying to justify why I haven't heard much from him.

"I told David I was coming here—I don't like to hide anything—but I told him it was just for three months. I'm a bit ashamed to tell him I stayed this long, a year. He did send me a little note, taped shut and enclosed in a neighbor's letter. He left it at her house, and she had someone bring it instead of mailing it. In that letter he told me he never thought I'd do such a thing as to tell him I was leaving for a short time and then not return. He was hurt by what I've done. He asked if I had decided to stay here, if I no longer wanted to live in Nicaragua. That hurt. It bothered me a lot. What could I say? Only that I came to get enough money to return. I told Alejandra to remind him again why I was here.

"He has meetings in Estelí, so for sure I'll see him when he comes to town. I don't have any illusions that we'll get back together. I know I'm the one to blame. It's already over. Maybe he has even another woman [besides the one he lives with]. What do I know? Maybe we can be friends. Maybe I can be a friend with the woman he lives with, too, friends but without her knowing that I was once his girlfriend. I don't think I'll go back to him. I don't know, not until I arrive will I be able to say the final word, not until I'm there.

"I'm trying to analyze the satisfaction we felt being together. I don't know if it's love. Maybe it was a need, the sexual satisfaction of meeting and making love. Or the excitement of going some place to eat, having two or three beers, and then going our separate ways. That was our life, and we managed to be together when we could. I try to reflect on it from here, and sometimes I think that everything I did with him, I did for the moment, out of necessity, or because I needed a man. But then I think, no, that wasn't it. I wanted to be with him, just to see him, to talk with him. I enjoyed his company, just knowing we could spend a moment together. Politically and sexually, we understand each other perfectly. I know the satisfaction is mutual. We adore talking together and making love.**"**

Six

Taking the VCR Back to Nicaragua

—I'll give you a month.

Yamileth and Miguel left for Nicaragua while I was still in Los Angeles. Their one-way LACSA (Línea Aérea Costarricense Sociedad Anónima, the Costa Rican airline) tickets were paid for by friends. On one side of the apartment, she lined up everything that was to go on the plane with her: ten boxes of used clothes, a television set, her prized used VCR, cheap dolls for the neighbor girls, five-dollar watches for the boys, the cream-colored *guayabera* shirt for David, a guitar someone had given her, sleeping bags, three VCR tapes already filled with comedies, and for Miguel his beloved baseball trophy, a bicycle, and a Nintendo game.[1]

Some of the items were luxuries in a Nicaraguan context, but they were also her hedges against inflation. When the Nicaraguan economy worsened, as it certainly would, some people would be willing to buy what she brought back. She tried to prepare herself for what inflation had done. A niece in Nicaragua, for example, was earning four million *córdobas* per day. Yamileth wondered what you bought with four million—maybe an egg or a pound of beans. She left three hundred dollars in a bank account in Oregon; I would send it to her as she needed it.

Yamileth hoped to tell people what life was like in the United States. Her sister-in-law, Irene, told her that when people had asked why Yamileth was returning, the only thing Irene could think of was to say that Miguel did not like it in the United States. Yamileth was committed to telling the truth when she returned, she said, about

---

[1]Yamileth saved most of the money that she had made working with Penny and Mark and used much of it to make her purchases before her return to Nicaragua. She bought a used VCR from Penny's mother.

how hard it was to get a job, how little you made, how many hours
you had to work, and how much everything cost.

We talked about the airport and the plane; she knew nothing
and wanted to know everything. It was all new: choosing seats (a
window seat for Miguel to see the sunrise), how to lock the bathroom door and flush the toilet (which brought laughter and embar-
rassment as we recalled the train trip), no need to pay for food
(would I please tell Miguel so that he would eat?), the little food
tray that pulls down (we laughed about the time I was served steak
and rice at six o'clock in the morning when leaving Managua), and
how she might be offered a drink (regrets over not flying the Nicaraguan airline and therefore not being able to drink the native rum,
Flor de Caña, which warmed up many U.S. travelers to Nicaragua).
She thought, as do many people, that Los Angeles would be a lot
closer to Managua than Miami; and if that were true, why did the
plane take longer to get there than it did from Miami? I told her to
take a sweater for the trip and how I had flown on such an old and
cold plane once from El Salvador that the passengers put on all
their clothes and could see their breath. She was as ready as I could
make her.

"Since I found out I'd leave in December, I've been marking off
the days on a little calendar. *'Ay, Dios mío,'* I say to myself, 'so
many days left!'

"But the trip has me worried. My only plane trip, to Cuba, was
years ago. I've never flown at night. We won't be able to see where
we are. I don't know what to do in the airport. Things like checking
in and having my luggage and papers looked at worry me. I wish
someone would do that for me so that all I had to do was get on the
plane. I'm always asking myself why I'm so worried. Those people
aren't going to stop me. They're not going to say, 'Stop here. We're
going to investigate you.' They're not going to run after me. I don't
know why but I'm afraid of the man who has those machines and
checks the things you take along, but I'll breathe easier when the
plane leaves.

"I'm nervous, but these nerves are going to stay here, parked at
the Los Angeles airport. The gangs will stay, too, and I'll be gone.
People who are just arriving can have those nerves, like an inheritance I saved for them.

"My fear about returning to Nicaragua is that I won't find a
way to get from the airport to Estelí. I sent a letter to Nilda, my
sister in Managua, another to Alejandra, and one to Irene, and I

told them I was coming without any money, but with some little things that'd make it impossible for me to get to Estelí by bus. I hope that among the three of them, especially Alejandra, they can figure out a way. If that doesn't work, I'll try to get a cargo truck to take me to Nilda's in Managua, but it's far from the airport, almost as far as it is to Estelí.

"So all that worries me, as do the changes that have taken place, like the currency—I don't know what anything is worth now—and maybe when you get off the plane with your little suitcase, they think you have a pile of dollars, so they beat you and rob you. When they see you with lots of luggage, they never think that the things you bring back have been given to you. So that worries me.

"It bothers me that lots of people will come to my house, not to see me but to see what I brought back, to see if I brought money. That's why I don't want to take anything home. I want to leave it in Managua and take only the television set to Estelí. That way, people will see that I returned with absolutely nothing. I'll also take with me the suitcase with little presents for everyone. Later, I'll bring the other things home.

"I know I'll be so tired I won't want to see anyone. I'll just want to rest. All in all, it'd be best if I arrived about nine o'clock at night. I'd go to my house, knock on the door, and say, 'Please open the door. Quietly. I'm tired.' I'd hide, and the next day I'd see everyone.

"If I come with a hundred dollars, it'll pay for the month's expenses and for my mother's anniversary. But I have to save whatever I can. I'll hide it in a spot where I can't lose it, and I won't change it to *córdobas* until it's necessary. If I arrived with a lot of money, people would ask me for it, some just to test me. I don't know if I'd be able to tell them no, although right now I think I could. People have written me asking for things. I say I'm barely making enough money to pay for the trip. They know I'll come back with nothing.

"Leticia said to me, 'Don't go. The future's here.'

" 'What future?' I asked. 'Tell me what future you have here and what future your children have. Give me some proof. Is being in debt having a future? Not being able to pay the rent? Not being able to buy food? Never having any rest, always running? Never spending one day with your children? That's the future?'

"She said, 'I'll give you a month. Then you'll call and ask me to bring you back.'

"I said, 'No!'

"I hope to change a little. That's one of my goals, but I don't know exactly what I'll change until I get there, just some things I've kept in my head. I'm going to try to feel good in my house and not be rude to anyone. I'm going to try to be more flexible with people. I want to change the way I've been overprotective with some people. I want to get to know people better. I'm going to try not to put my life on the line so much in dangerous zones. And I'm going to try not to get so upset. If I find work, I'm going to spend more time than before making sure my son studies and learns a trade. I want to make him less attached to me, make him feel useful without my help.

"Leticia told me that Miguel wanted to stay here and that I wouldn't let him. I was angry. He never used to say things to others about me. 'So, Miguel,' I asked, 'why did you tell your aunt that you wanted to stay here and I wouldn't let you?'

" 'I haven't said anything,' he replied. 'I do want to go. I don't want to stay.' She lied, not he. Miguel understands that he's not staying here. He knows it's not possible. We've talked about the chance he may be drafted in Nicaragua, and he still wants to go. If he has to join the military, so be it. It depends on the situation. Miguel's my only child, so maybe he won't have to go. I have a little advantage because I know some people, heads of delegations, let's say, and I can talk with someone. It's not right to do that, and certainly no one is going to speak up for the *campesinos*. No one would even listen to them. They have to go where they're sent. So I'd feel bad about doing it. Still, I'd ask them, since he's my only child, if they have to take him. If it's really necessary, take him, but if not, let him work and help me at home. On the other hand, I'd like him to have the military preparation so he'd see how life really is. I know it's still difficult there. We all could die, or he could live and I die. You can't predict anything.**"**

We talked about Nicaragua's future. I said that I did not think that anything good would happen soon in Nicaragua, maybe in a hundred years. Yamileth laughed and said, "In a hundred years? Do you really think it will happen then?" I next asked what the future held for her in Nicaragua. She took a deep breath and chose her words carefully and deliberately.

"The future means I'll be in my own country to work and develop myself however I can, but the future depends on the job I find and whatever presents itself. I don't think we'll always live in war, in conflict, like we do now. Since I've been in Los Angeles, people I know have died. The ones who are left alive will have a better life and will be more careful about whom they elect to the government. Maybe we'll learn how to administer the country through the errors we've made. We have faith, most of us do.

"I don't know where I'll work because I don't have the whole picture of life there. People have told me it's bad, very difficult, hard to get food. The good thing is that the family will be together, like bees, little by little going to our home.

"I do worry a little, though, about what people have been saying. Omar told me that rumors have already started. He said, 'Your neighbor—the one you sent shoes to—is talking about you. But don't pay any attention to her. It doesn't matter.' I really don't worry much about her. She always does things like that. I don't know why, but they talk all the time.

"I think people should help when there's something to do, but they shouldn't tell people how to live their lives. Your life is your own life, not someone else's. Let people do what they want to do. I don't visit someone just so I can talk about them. When people start gossiping, I change the conversation and say that I'm sorry. I try to control it, just as my mother did. How important to me is a neighbor? She's important only when she needs a pill. Her private life is hers. No one in the United States even knows the names of their neighbors. If the mailman asked where someone lived, no one would have any idea. In some ways, that's better."

Yamileth and Miguel had wanted me to go with them to the airport—the round-trip drive to the airport took two hours and their plane left after midnight—but I had finished my chemotherapy only two months before and simply did not have the energy to accompany her. She said that she needed "someone legal to tell her what to do," but it had to be someone else. Boyfriends of her nieces took them, but the rest of the family stayed home since they had heard that *la migra* patrolled the airport heavily.

Yamileth came to the hotel to say goodbye, wobbling on new three-inch heels, wearing a bright sky-blue suit, long pink false fingernails, makeup, and styled hair. It was the drop-dead look, a combination of the style of a moneyed Latin American woman and a Southern California one. Such was her determination to go back looking good that she had agreed to be "made over" by her nieces. She had come a long way from the border crossing of almost a year ago.

Before she left, she said, "The worst thing that could happen to me would be to lose everything I'm bringing back, the things as well as the money. Then I'd have no way to solve my problems." I assured her that she and Miguel would not miss their plane during their stopover in the San José, Costa Rica, airport and warned her to avoid the women customs agents in Nicaragua, who always seemed to be the least forgiving. I told her to take along her birth control pills (I had always reminded her to take them when I left Nicaragua), and we said good-bye. Yamileth teetered out the door on her way back to her native land.

~

Yamileth and Miguel landed safely in Managua on December 8, 1989. Their plane had been delayed for twelve hours in San José, so no one was waiting for them at the Nicaraguan airport. Omar, who had been released from house arrest for the arrival, had waited for her along with Irene, but they had given up and gone back to Estelí, leaving Yamileth, still in her three-inch heels, to find her way to Nilda's in Managua.

None of their checked-in luggage arrived. The Oregon bat, the Nintendo game, the used clothes, David's *guayabera* shirt, the VCR, and the bicycle had vanished somewhere between the Los Angeles and Managua airports—everything that they had bought and been given. Yamileth no longer had to worry about showing up in Estelí with enough boxes to create gossip. She returned as she had left, empty-handed, except for what they had in their carry-on bags and the television set that they had kept with them. Fortunately, Miguel had taken the Lake Oswego baseball trophy in his backpack, so he still had that memento.

A couple of months later, in February 1990, Violeta Chamorro defeated the Sandinista candidate, Daniel Ortega, in the Nicaraguan elections. I called Yamileth, who was surprised by the result but thought that the Sandinistas would continue to be a major force "by governing from below," as she put it. The Sandinistas would make sure that Chamorro fulfilled her campaign promises. Yamileth maintained that the victory was attained by buying votes for as little as two dollars and as much as fifty.

Meanwhile, in Estelí, one of the few places where the Sandinistas had beaten Chamorro's party, tension grew and gunshots could be heard again. Her ideas would not change, Yamileth said, and she still believed that she belonged to the strongest party, the Sandinistas. She laughed and sounded confident. She was the old Yamileth, looking for ways to help schools, *campesinos*, and cooperatives.

She asked me to send fifty dollars from her Corvallis account so that she could buy beans and rice. She had filed a claim with the airline for her luggage, and they settled it by giving her one ticket to Los Angeles. She volunteered part-time for the Sandinistas, much as she had always done. And David? Yes, she still saw him, even though he was still with the woman. And she laughed again.

And Gustavo, the man who had come to visit her in Los Angeles? She had been so sure that she would find out what he had been up to. The scoundrel, she said, had embezzled money from the Sandinistas and did not represent State Security. He was not at all what he had intimated that he was; instead, he was a criminal.

A few weeks later, Yamileth called to ask me to send another fifty dollars. She was worried that Violeta, whom she usually referred to as "she," would take away her house because the Sandinistas had never compensated the original owner for the land. The bravado and laughter of the first call were gone.

It was September 1990 when I received the next call. She was desperate, she said. The military had been cut back, and Omar had lost his job. Before the election, he had been with the army in the mountains and had gone for a week without sleep. He then began drinking and later was told that there was no more work for him in the army, so he had to leave. It broke him. He had been in the hospital for a month with his recurring posttraumatic stress disorder.[2]

Nicaraguans talked about a civil war. Every Saturday the *córdoba* was devalued. The Ministry of Health had not paid anyone for two months, and Yamileth thought that the employees would strike. The Sandinistas still had meetings in the barrio, but the fact that they no longer met in the city center symbolized their loss of power. They said that things would get better, but Yamileth doubted it. I asked if she still went to the meetings, and she said, "When I can. Sometimes yes and sometimes no."

---

[2] Joel Garfunkel, a psychologist at the Corvallis Clinic, read Omar's history in 1985 and concluded that his symptoms were consistent with those of posttraumatic stress disorder. Such symptoms often intensify when individuals are exposed to situations that resemble the original trauma. Omar's trauma came from being at war, either with the Somoza guards, the Contras, or a mixture thereof, for much of his life.

No one had any work. She had helped a woman sell used clothes, but now the woman had left the country. Irene washed clothes in the river, but not many could afford to pay her, and she did not make enough money to feed the family. It was just like the days under Somoza. Yamileth asked me to send the remaining two hundred dollars.

Around the middle of December 1990, Yamileth and Miguel flew to Los Angeles, using the one ticket that LACSA had given her and selling the television set for the other one. They arrived with legal documents for a six-month stay, obtained by telling the U.S. embassy in Managua that Miguel needed medical care. Later, when I asked her about her resolutions to make changes in her life, she would tell me only that they had left Nicaragua out of hunger.

They stayed with Leticia, and Yamileth worked much as she had before and at the same time made plans to return to Oregon. Gangs still threatened them—each had fought off attacks—and when Penny and Mark heard about their troubles, they once more opened their home to them. They were especially concerned about Miguel's education. Once again, Yamileth did not take them up on their offer.

Six months later, still in Los Angeles, their visas expired and Immigration officials told them that they would have to leave the States. If they did so and then returned, they would be given a six-month extension on their visas. Yamileth and Miguel took what money they had saved, borrowed the rest, and flew back to Nicaragua in mid-May 1991. A few weeks later, when they returned to Los Angeles as planned, she said that, as usual, Omar was sick and there was no work for anyone and no food. Yamileth, too, had had trouble in Nicaragua; she no longer had her monthly periods, as often happened when she was under stress. True to the official word, she could stay in the United States for another six months.

Seven

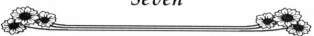

Love and Baking

—We're open all the time, or so it seems.

"**D**avid and I were together as much as we could be. At the end, he didn't know I was coming back to the United States, and I didn't know I was pregnant, and that's why he still doesn't know."

The pregnancy put pressure on Yamileth in many ways, and certainly she needed to resolve her financial situation. She made arrangements to buy a bakery in a Pico-Union shopping plaza. Since her return from Nicaragua in June, she had been working there, arriving every morning at four o'clock and staying until late in the evening. When I called, she would drop her voice with the hope that her boss would not hear and whisper to me a number in the range of seventy-five thousand dollars. I kept asking, "What do you know about baking?" She would answer that she was learning. I would add, "See a lawyer," and she said that she would.

In August, she signed a contract with the Salvadoran owner of the bakery in which she agreed that if the bakery failed, it would revert to him. Each month she would pay him for the business, pay the Cuban building manager for the rent—which he in turn gave to the Korean building owner—and pay the Guatemalan baker. Yamileth's first entrepreneurial venture was a Nicaraguan bakery, but a distinctly Los Angeles version.

The family, including Marisa's new husband, Manuel, moved into the first floor of a house in South-Central Los Angeles. Their neighbors were African-American renters in attractive low-income apartments. They could see the University of Southern California from the end of their sidewalk and shop at the Sorbonne Plaza just up the street. It was a quiet neighborhood, and the family hoped that they would be safer. The two-story stucco house with purple jacarandas and blue hydrangeas blooming out front bore an uncanny resemblance to their Nicaraguan home with its leafy plants and bamboo. However, the area was neither secure nor lively enough for me to imagine Doña María sitting on the porch talking to anyone who passed by. Marisa and Manuel had one bedroom, Leticia and the girls had the other, a cousin slept in a makeshift bedroom carved out of the dining room, and Yamileth and Miguel slept on the L-shaped living-room couch. Another renter lived upstairs. Leticia and Sofía eventually moved away to be nearer to their work, but this house, a grown-up and fat U.S. version of the one that they had left behind, was home to everyone.

Yamileth was ten minutes by car and a half-hour by bus from the bakery. Almost from the beginning, Manuel, who was from Mexico and had legal papers, worked with Yamileth. His amiability, complemented by a big, open smile and dimples in his cheeks, eased his welcome into the family, and the English he knew helped in the bakery.

The Pico-Union shopping plaza housed small restaurants, the beauty salon where Leticia and Marisa worked, a small grocery store, an immigration lawyer's office, and, behind closed doors and papered-up windows, sweatshops full of Asian women sewing clothes. The bakery's neon sign read, "Bakery Open 24 Hours a Day," but when I asked the family about that, everyone laughed. "With the *cholos* and *pandillas*, all the gangs around here? You must be kidding!"

Nora and Miguel identified the pastries: mid-sized and small *quesadillas*; pineapple-, cream-, and apple-stuffed *empanadas*; a coffee cake called *marquesota*; sweet or plain *roscas*, a cookie with red sugar on the top that they called a *peperrecha*; crescent-shaped rolls called *cachitos*; cream-filled Guatemalan cupcakes called *crescas*; rolls with chocolate on the top; a bread named *salpor* with either rice or flour on the top indicating the main ingredient. Most of the time they did not know the names, making them up or guessing at them as we went along the glass case.

Yamileth made plans to redecorate. The garbanzo, pinto, and black beans in three large plastic barrels near the entrance would be moved some day to make way for a small counter and stools. The MS. PAC-MAN video game, so defined by an egg-shaped person with pink bows and shapely legs, would stay, and so would the straggly *piñata* placed on the top. A nearly empty cooler on the far wall offered soda, boxes of Farmer John lard, white and chocolate milk, a piña colada yogurt, and a handful of limes. On top of the cooler were a few boxes of Minute Rice, Cheerios, Aunt Jemima pancake mix, and Gerber oatmeal, lonely cans of anchovies, Teasdale white hominy for *posole*, and jars of Coffee-mate and Wesson oil. Lined up on another shelf were bags of Los Pericos tostadas, cans of Enfamil, Van Camp pork and beans, and Hunt's chili beans. A previous owner had left a rack of Chulada spices, herbs, and snacks ranging from simple cake decorations to more exotic ground shrimp, orange blossoms, cane sugar, and hibiscus tea bags.

As Yamileth stood behind the bakery counter, the harsh fluorescent lighting made her look tired and drawn, even more so next to tall and stocky Manuel. Marisa had experimented with a red color on Yamileth's hair and had straightened her curls. Her light green maternity dress with tiny white figures matched the delicateness of her condition, and a mask of pregnancy showed clearly on her ruddy skin.

Everyone in the family, from the youngest to the oldest, worked in the bakery. If you walked in and knew the family, you soon stood behind the counter selling Central American sweet bread and rolls. In their moments of leisure, the children played on the floor, did their homework in the corners, and watched television on a small set. Boyfriends visited, and there was always someone to talk with. In the back, tucked away from the ovens, was a mattress where Yamileth napped. The bakery brought the family together. The old household complaints—not helping enough, eating too much, expecting too much—halted as the family members took on new roles in their joint venture.

"During this warm weather, we haven't sold much. We have to change something. We just don't have enough experience, so we're watching the bakery fall apart. The owner, who wants us to succeed, told us that we were going to have these problems and said that things would improve in the winter when it gets cooler. But right now we're struggling along.

"We're open all the time, or so it seems. The baker has only Sundays off, so on Saturdays he works longer hours. Still, we keep the bread fresh on Sundays, as if it just came out of the oven. People come in and say, 'It looks so fresh!' Manuel and I work from six o'clock in the morning Sundays until eight o'clock at night, but the other six days of the week, it's from five to ten, sixteen hours a day, way too much.

"I've heard rumors that the owner has regretted signing the contract with me and wants it back, but we don't want to do that. Let's get through this ninety-degree weather first. If things are good in the winter, then we can make plans for the summer, like having sodas, ice cream, seasonal things like *horchata* [a cold drink made of almonds]. We've made nothing, no money at all, only what we need to keep the bakery going. We're barely hanging on.

"Not all the people who shop in the bakery speak Spanish. I understand them, but the problem is telling them the prices. I know some numbers in English but not all of them, so I have to write it down. Lots of Chinese come in—*¡Híjole madre!*—and then I don't understand anything! They come early in the morning, all at once, and leave just as suddenly. I use gestures and a piece of paper, and they always know how much change to expect."

~

"When David and I were together in Nicaragua, we understood each other, as always. We've agreed to be together without commitment, to take advantage of the moment, and nothing more. There is no commitment on his part or on mine. We have always lived for the moment, sharing the days of work, the happiness, all that. It went well for us. We understood each other perfectly.

"The problem right now is that I haven't written anything to him about the pregnancy. I don't know why. I can't explain it to myself. There are moments when I want to write him, but then I don't do it. No, it's not that I want him to *do* something—the only thing he could do is write, not daily, but write—but what I do want is for everything to turn out well. If it does, then I'll send him photos from the time I went to the doctor until the birth. If the baby is healthy, then, yes, I'll tell him. But if not, well, why would I tell him something right now if I don't know how we're going to be? That's what I tell the children: Don't build up your hopes—although they already have—about the new baby because no one knows what's going to happen. Only God knows, so we should wait. Buy nothing, *nada de nada*. Underwear is more than sufficient for a child who's not yet born."

In November I went out for dinner with Leticia, who, after we ordered, wasted no time when she said, "Let's get down to business." Yamileth was pregnant, and no one knew who the father was, and Yamileth would not tell anyone. Leticia said that when Marisa suggested that it might be a *gringo* whom Yamileth had gone out with before she left for Nicaragua, all Yamileth did was laugh. When I suggested to Leticia that it might be a Nicaraguan, Leticia shook her head no and said that Alejandra had told her that the only boyfriend Yamileth had, "the love of her life," had earlier been killed in a motorcycle accident. That was all news to me.

The problem was the date. If the baby was due on January 26, 1992, as the doctors said, Yamileth had been in the United States at the time of conception, which is also why my suggestion to Leticia that the father may be a Nicaraguan was dismissed. I knew, though, or thought I knew. It was David. The dates might be slightly off, but I believed Yamileth. And the love of her life dying in a motorcycle accident? I asked. She had never heard of such a story. Besides, at that moment she was more concerned about the bakery.

Yamileth lost the bakery the day after Christmas, 1991. A short time later, Los Angeles experienced one of its coldest and wettest winters, which, sadly enough, if she had managed to hang on, might have brought the promised increase in business. It had been an exciting, risky, and brave venture for everyone, and they all were deeply disappointed.

"Sometimes when we're all happy, we get together and laugh about the bakery. Just the other day we were all lying on the floor and looking back, laughing as if we had won the lottery. We talked about when we got up so early, when we raced to the bus, or when I had to run there alone, afraid of the gangs. I was scared even when I was dressing, listening for footsteps. *¡Híjole!* And Marisa said, 'And I was so tired that I slept in the car when I rode to the bakery with Manuel!' We laugh because otherwise, we'd just be disgusted. Now we use the experience as a diversion.

"We thought about our trip from Nicaragua to California and all the difficulties, leaving Estelí, traveling from one country to another to get here, hiding along the way, finally arriving at the tiny apartment, only to sleep on the floor! Since we didn't know what was waiting for us, we began to work and struggle and then bought some small mattresses to sleep on. We continued to improve things and here we are, with a house, and everything is fine— *gracias a Dios*—except for this little problem of the bakery. Another failure. You have to think about how to go on without getting too tired to do it. If we let desperation overcome us, we'd go crazy and never find a way out.

"Still, we've been successful, more or less, with short bursts of happiness. Talk about short-lived, I didn't even make fifty cents from the bakery! It was a fantasy. I dreamed of a theater where I was going to do something wonderful, and then I woke up and realized I didn't do anything. All of us imagined that we were going to do something together, but it turned out that our theater fell apart. Manuel didn't make a penny, and neither did I. All we got was a lot of work and little sleep, making only enough money to pay the rent, to pay the baker, to pay the lights.

"We started the bakery in August and the problems began by November. In September we received a three-hundred-dollar bill for lights. We said to each other that since we were working the machines longer each day, that's why it came out high. So we talked with the baker and stopped the air conditioning, turned off the fruit cooler, and economized our use of electricity. But it didn't work. The bill turned out even higher even though we didn't have everything running. We couldn't figure out why it got higher when we kept turning everything off! It increased to more than five hundred, then to more than two thousand, and, since we owed some, the last month it reached three thousand dollars.

"A man from the power company put a note on our switch saying that we had to leave it on—it lit a room on the other side of the bakery—because if we turned it off, the public phones in front of the bakery wouldn't work. When I asked why it worked like that, they said that the owner of the building knew the system, that they had no arrangement with us, rather with the owner. We almost never saw the owner, only the manager who rented it to us. He said he was going to find out, but he never did. So we owed three thousand. I didn't pay it. I couldn't. I simply couldn't!

"At one time, our expenses were more than seven thousand dollars. We spent fifteen hundred monthly on materials, six to five hundred a month on the baker, and a thousand to fourteen hundred a month went for the rent, depending on expenses. I remember doing the accounts with Marisa one day, and it turned out to be eight thousand five hundred dollars. *¡Híjole!* We didn't know what to do when we saw a number so large. Eight thousand five hundred! *¡Híjole madre!* To pay bills that large, Marisa often had to take money out of her salary. She'd say, 'Take this. I'll lend it to you to buy cream,' but we never repaid her, and that makes me sad. During the last days, when we were to pay the baker, we had no more than a hundred dollars. There was nothing to do. Marisa came and said, 'Take this to pay him.'

"We never had the pleasure of saying, 'Let's go to a restaurant,' or 'Let's buy a pair of shoes' with anything we earned. We couldn't buy a pair of underpants, not even a pair of the cheapest socks that cost one dollar, not a ninety-nine-cent bottle of shampoo for my unborn child. And on top of that, I worried that people would be unhappy with me and that the power company would put me in prison.

"Every day, even the last one, I got up at four o'clock in the morning to go to work. Fortunately, we didn't owe anything to the man who charged the rent or to the baker who worked for us. I talked to the bakery owner and said, 'Look, we're going to give back the business because I really can't do it. I'm sick, the pregnancy isn't going well, I don't sleep, there's a lot of work, and I'm going to give it back if that's all right with you.'

" 'Look, *hija*,' he said, 'if you want to get the business back when things are better for you, come look for me.'

" 'Fine,' I said, but I still wanted to return it. I didn't go back to see his face because it made me ashamed. I don't know if they cut off the lights. I didn't find out. I didn't return. I received the bakery with lights, water, everything functioning, and returned it working the same as when I received it. I haven't seen him. I haven't shown up there, ever, ever, ever!

"In spite of that, though, we've had bursts of happiness, the sort that when you think you've reached the sky, you end up on the floor again. New experiences, but good ones. Leticia has started a new salon, and she and I now think that God didn't want each business, hers and mine, to turn out the same. If things go poorly for Leticia in her salon, she has to figure out what to do. My contract, however, said that mine would return to the owner."

A month after they lost the bakery, on January 27, 1992, Yamileth gave birth to her daughter and my namesake, Diana María, at Los Angeles County-USC Medical Center in Los Angeles. María, of course, had been Yamileth's mother's name. How astonished she would have been to have a grandchild born in the United States!

Yamileth's visa had expired a few weeks before. She had hoped to be able to extend it legally, but after checking with an immigration lawyer, she had decided that to do so was too risky. She was once more in the country without legal documentation.

"The hospital experience makes me laugh now, but at the time I didn't laugh because I was afraid. But even then it was funny, mainly because Marisa was laughing. All those women walking in the hall, walking and walking. One would be coming this way and I'd be going the other; and suddenly, when the pain came, one of us would grab the wall. Marisa laughed and said we were holding up the wall so that it wouldn't fall down.

"I continued to walk the hall with the women, and every half hour or fifteen minutes, the doctors and nurses would check me. I never found out what it was that worried them, and I never knew why they examined me so often and why they kept asking me, 'How do you feel? Is the baby moving?'[1] Three doctors were taking care of me, along with two nurses, and they were with me all the time, and later a midwife, too. Supposedly the baby was on one side, tried to come out but went back in, and ended up turned around and unable to get out. The doctors were worried. With their help, I got to one side; and when the pain came, they told me to push. I asked the Virgin to help me so that the baby wouldn't come out deformed, with problems. When Diana was born, they put her to my breast. The doctors and the midwife and the nurses were all there—so happy—and everyone held Diana, a little bit for each of them. I had never thought they would treat me so well. I was afraid because I had heard that they behaved badly toward people who weren't important to them, but I can say that it was just the opposite.[2]

"I think she looks like her father. Leticia thinks she looks like Miguel and like Marisa when she was little. The family still doesn't know who the father is. They've asked me, but I told them that if they really want to help me, one of the conditions is not to talk about that, only do the normal things, peacefully, with no questions. Now they don't ask. That was the agreement, and they've all gone along with it.

"Before the baby was born, I didn't want them to buy anything, not a crib, not clothes, nothing, because I was afraid of dying. Let's suppose I lived and the child died, and they had bought these things? That would be painful, so it was better not to buy anything. 'No, Tía,' they'd say, 'you have to struggle and have the strength to say that all is going to come out well. We are going to have a baby boy

---

[1] The exact cause for concern is unknown. It may have been related to her advanced maternal age but more likely was concern about an intrapartum problem, such as unusual fetal position, fetal heart-rate irregularities, or slow cervical dilation.

[2] Yamileth was probably in a high-risk maternity ward where the patient-physician ratio is relatively low.

or girl here with us, so don't say those things.' Everyone took care of me, 'Don't do that, *Tía*. Careful, *Tía*. Take this pill, *Tía*. You're not going to die, *Tía*, you're not in Nicaragua. The doctors will take care of you even though you can't pay.'

"At the same time, Miguel worries me. I know he feels rejected. Instead of hanging around to talk with everyone as he used to do, he stays isolated, as if nothing is important to him. And the girls liked to annoy him by saying, 'Your mama is going to have a pretty little girl. She'll be an American and you're going to always be the same old wetback.'

"Life here isn't easy. It made Miguel nervous to be in the bakery and have fifteen, twenty, twenty-five members of a gang outside, throwing things at cars and buses and spray-painting them. I could have turned them in, but for what? For the money? They'd be back on the streets the next day, looking for me.

"The only English Miguel likes is in music. Can you imagine? He likes the music here now more than Latin American music! His school [Canoga Park High School] is so far away that I have no contact with it, but I know he doesn't do well. And no, he doesn't ever play baseball. I don't know why. And when he's afraid to go to school, I don't send him."

~

"[It is May and] I still haven't told David about Diana. I can't send him a letter; maybe it wouldn't get there, or it might end up with someone else. The best way is through my friend Alejandra because she knows how to get it to him directly. I sent her photographs of Diana, so if he has talked with her, he knows. But I don't know what happened because she's in the hospital.

"Several months ago she asked me to send her some money for an operation, but I was in a bad situation with that bakery and couldn't send more than five dollars with a person going to Nicaragua.[3] It worries me that I haven't received an answer because I don't know if she's well or not. I've even dreamed that she died. I love her a lot. She loved my mother and helped us financially when the situation was difficult. Now that she needs me, I can't do any more for her other than ask her how she is.

---

[3]For Yamileth and her family the usual way of corresponding with friends and family in Nicaragua is by sending letters and packages with people whose job it is to go back and forth delivering items.

"I still plan to return to Nicaragua some day, but I have no plans to make a home with David. He has his commitments, although I don't know how he feels about them. I know that matrimony should last forever, especially for the children's sake, but it's also possible that it doesn't. We'll see. My idea is to return for good, to talk with him if I have the opportunity, and to be with him if we don't have problems. We've already agreed that we'll always be friends and we'll always visit each other."

Eight

Just Being with Them Makes Me Happy

—My two little black ones . . .

"I used to feel so empty, especially last fall when I was pregnant, but now I don't. I give infinite thanks to God and to the help that I've received from Marisa, from Manuel, and from everyone around me. One way or another, they've supported me. They love Diana, and just being with her makes me happy.

"I do have problems with my son, who's jealous. He says that everyone brings Diana presents but not him. 'Marisa gives presents to the baby and not to me,' he complains, 'and Manuel picks her up and plays with her.' I grab my son and I tease both of them, Diana and Miguel. '*Ay*, my two little black ones, *mis negritos*,'[1] I tell them, 'it's so beautiful to have my two black ones.' I try to distribute the love evenly, but even Nora is jealous and says contemptuously about Diana, 'Now they don't love me, only her.'

"Miguel loves to squeeze Diana and wants her to be big enough to walk. She still has to be treated delicately, but they don't do that. No one in the house treats her with tenderness. Instead, they act as if she's a child of two years. It frightens me, but, at the same time, I can't say no because I could lose those who love me. I worry, though, when she's sleeping here with me on the couch. I almost never sleep. I worry because on television they say many children die. They don't know the cause, but they turn up dead. So I lie there all night making sure she breathes. Leticia laughs because

---

[1]*Negrito*, as Yamileth uses it, is a term of endearment. Her neighbors in Estelí had often called her *Negrita*, and she in turn uses the name with her children. When she referred to African Americans, she usually chose the word *moreno*, which means brown.

she wonders how I sleep without falling off the couch. I put Diana on the inside and I take the outside. The reason I don't fall is that I lie on the edge, awake and worrying about her. It's an L-shaped couch, and Miguel sleeps on the other end. Our feet cross. Sometimes we start playing at night and he tickles me. He often wants the three of us to sleep on one side, but I tell him, 'That's impossible. Why don't we sleep on the floor instead?' One night we tried it, but Diana didn't like it.

"But no, I no longer have that emptiness. I'm happy. I have a strong commitment to Marisa, more than anyone, because it's she who has to take care of the food. If Diana has an appointment one day, Marisa doesn't go to work or tells Manuel that he has to get up early to take me to the clinic. When the family hears Diana cry, they're concerned, attentive, so I have much to be thankful for. So I try to keep the house clean, to help them with many things, to have food for them when I can. In that way I can pay back what they're doing, not just for my daughter but for my son and for me, too.

"I tell Marisa that we need to buy beans and rice—that's what's most necessary—and, when we have some extra money, we buy meat or chicken, but always we have Nicaraguan rice and beans, *gallo pinto*. Morning, noon, afternoon, or night, someone is always here wanting to eat it.

"For myself, I have no money to spend. Anyhow, I don't go out in the street, partly because I'm afraid if I go with my daughter that they might take her from me or something will happen. I don't know, there are so many things in my mind that I, instead of maturing, have become more childlike for fear of something happening to my daughter. So I don't go. I prefer to call Marisa and say, 'Marisa, if you have money, bring such and such a thing, *chiltomá* [a sweet green pepper and a medicinal herb, possibly for tea] or mint.' Whatever spices I might need, she gets when she can.

"Some days are more difficult than others, but I have faith that God will help Marisa and that Manuel will find a job because those two don't want me to look for work and take the child. There's no one around here to leave her with. They're all African Americans, and African Americans don't have confidence in anyone besides themselves.

"One day I went shopping on Miguel's bike, and I rode fast because I had left Diana with him. On the corner I met up with a man who wanted me to get off the bike and give it to him. I understood what he wanted but I said, 'No speaking English.' He tried to take it from me, but I pushed him away. He followed me to the store, but I asked the clerk if he would let me put my bike in the store. At every moment you have to be ready because they'll take your shoes right off you.

"I've always had the idea of returning to Nicaragua but not right now, not tomorrow, nor the morning after. A reason to stay in the United States was to have had my daughter here. They took good care of me and gave both my daughter and me good medical care without it costing a cent. They told me that I'd have to pay it back, little by little. I'm sure that if I find a good job, I'll do it, especially with a conscience like mine. All medicines are available here, and everything is easier.

"Miguel is supposed to be going to Belmont High School, but I'm frightened to let him go. He left Canoga Park High School because he thought that the gangs would catch him and make him do something by force. He left, not out of fear, but out of terror. I know that it's important for him to go to school, but I'm afraid of losing him. In one month, four children have died in Los Angeles from stray bullets. That kind of tension makes you nervous. Maybe I feel it more than others because I've seen so much in Los Angeles and in my country. Having seen so many things . . . it's another tension, maybe a little different, but with the same fear of losing a loved one. The tension never ends. People say they're not safe at home, not at work, and not in the streets. It's just best not to go out.

"It's gotten even more dangerous in our old neighborhood on Bonnie Brae [just north of Pico Boulevard]. There still are barricades in the streets, but it's more closed, not possible for anything to enter, no cars. It's sealed off with permanent posts put in the ground. It's the most secure measure. No longer do cars enter, and the people who come into the neighborhood have criminal records and are known to be buying and distributing drugs. Only people enter, no cars.

"My visa has expired now. People tell me I can get false documents, but I've been afraid to do that because *la migra* can catch me. They say I can deceive the government, though, but what I can't do is deceive myself. My conscience tells me not to. Besides, they'd find out and that would make me more ashamed. I don't want anyone in Nicaragua to say that we did anything dishonest. It's better to stay quietly undocumented, quietly looking for work, and not doing things we shouldn't.''

~

"Alejandra called [in September] to ask how I was. She realized that I had had the baby and she wanted to talk with me. I had no idea that David was at her side when she called. She asked, 'How's the baby? Well?'

" 'Yes, of course. I sent you some photos. Did you get them?'

" 'Yes, I did,' she said, and then added, 'Listen, someone you know was killed in an ambush.'

" 'David?'

" 'Yes, David.'

" 'I don't believe you.'

" 'It's true, and you know who he was with? All those friends who hang around with him.'

"I didn't believe her.

"Suddenly she burst into laughter. 'Yes, I'm lying! Don't believe me! Do you want to talk with him?' And she put him on the line.

"He told me that he was fine and asked when I was going to return. We talked for a long time—fifteen minutes—and he told me he was no longer in the military because there had been another cutback with the new president. He was planting rice on his land— he has quite a bit—with his mother and brothers in Jalapa. He's also working for the Farm Workers Association [Asociación de Trabajadores del Campo] by organizing the workers in the field, just like a good Sandinista. That makes me happy because I told him that in spite of what happens, he shouldn't let anything take away the ideas we fought for. I was chatting with him, talking politically, and he explained to me that we need to give the Sandinista Front the strength to rise up again and return to power. It will be difficult, he said, but we had to figure out how to do it.

"Both of them, David and Alejandra, want me to return. I would like to go back, I would, but the problem is that I have to consider my children, especially Diana. She's young, and I worry about her food. They're offering me work, again related to the women's association, but they couldn't promise that I'd make a nice salary, or even enough to pay the water bill, the electricity, and buy food for Diana. Work satisfies me a lot. I love it, especially since I'd be doing what I love to do, but the pay is too little. I just don't think it would be enough. If I went back, though, I'd live in Estelí so we wouldn't see each other every day. But when we'd meet, it would go on for a week!

"The situation in Nicaragua is like it is everywhere. There's food, but you need money to buy it. Here in the United States there are so many things to buy, but how can you buy them without money? Here I feel more tension, so much so that it makes me want to cry, and I feel a desperateness because I'm not doing anything. I mean, even though I'm doing a lot—I clean the house and cook after I come home from working in the beauty salon. I wash people's hair, comb it out, and spray it so that it's ready for Marisa to work on. Some people come for permanents and need a treatment. Marisa says, 'Look, *Tía*, put the treatment on that woman, and put this woman under the dryer for so many minutes,' and I do it. Sometimes, we have only two clients a day; but last Saturday, six people came at eight o'clock in the morning to get ready for the *quinceñera*, the celebration [of a teenage girl] for being fifteen years old. The other day, though, no one came. So we have ups and downs here, too, just as in Nicaragua.

"Yes, I used to think that by being with David, I was doing something that hurt the other woman, that damaged women throughout the world. But now I don't know. Being there, looking at things to see if it's the same or isn't . . . I mean, I have those feelings, but not when I'm there! When I'm there, I don't know if that's true. Look, I know it's not right to share him or to make life impossible for her because then neither one of us will feel secure about what we have. I, for example, have never had the idea that he would be with me for all of my life. I have lived with the idea that I'll have him with me when I can, and he'll be with me when he can, and I feel good about that. But then, again, I don't know. The only problem is if she realizes that he wants to see me. I would try not to go there, but if I have to work there, I have to go, but I don't want to cause problems with her, nor cause problems for the work I'd be doing. The Farm Workers Association has regional meetings there every couple of weeks, depending on what we're planning. I'd have to go—maybe to take care of something personally! But no, I don't feel sure of him. No, no.

"David found out about Diana because I sent him some photographs through Alejandra. I didn't know that she had been elected to be AMNLAE's regional director and thought she was still working in a school. She wrote to me about her operation and that she might lose her job, but four months later she wrote to me about her new position and asked me when I wanted to come. Before that, I had sent her a letter with the photos and she took them to Jalapa. That's how David found out. I had written just a few words to him on a sheet, all stapled shut, because I wasn't sure if it would get to him or if Alejandra was going to be able to see him. I thought she was still teaching and had to spend all week in the school, which would leave her with no pretext to visit Jalapa. But, as it turns out, with her new job she travels throughout the region.

"Yes, he was happy. He could hear Diana, so I put her on the phone so he could talk with her and hear her. It made him happy, and her, too.

"The family still doesn't know about David. All they know is that I brought Diana from Nicaragua—and they don't even believe that! That I do not like, but it's their problem, not mine."

Nine

Thoughts Along the Way

Cultural Differences

Life in the United States surprised Yamileth at times, but her good humor took her through the awkward moments. I remember watching her one day as she approached a sink that had faucets that even those of us who have always lived here would consider unusual. She stood back and looked at the faucets, then slowly and deliberately reached out and lifted the main one. It worked! Next, she turned it to the right and felt the water, then to the left. She stepped back and smiled. She had been surprised by hot water in the pipes, toilets that accepted toilet paper, supermarkets where the meat was all cut up and prepackaged, as well as by people sleeping under bridges, begging on the street, and going through the garbage. And for sure, she said, no one in Nicaragua would believe how much rent she had to pay.

Our behavior, though, sometimes left her (and me) astonished, as she recounted in the following tale: "I went to a little café in Los Angeles where they sell *gallo pinto* with cream that tastes the same as in Nicaragua. I went with Leticia and some other people, and we ate quickly. Before we finished, I stood up. I left a little on my plate that I intended to come back and finish. But some drunks came in, and even though the people in the restaurant tried to stop this man, one of them managed to grab my plate and run out with it. Shamelessly! I've never seen that in Nicaragua—that someone would come in and take my food!" In general, however, Yamileth saw many similarities to her homeland:

> Life is much the same. People work, eat, do their daily chores. There are more sophisticated things in the United States, though. For example, most of us don't have washers and dryers in Nicaragua. We wash by hand and dry in the sun. . . . At the same time,

I noticed—in your part of Oregon, not in Los Angeles—that you can leave your things on the porch or on the grass, and no one touches them. No one worries that someone, out of malice, will take them. No one is worried about material things. There's not much corruption in Oregon, not on the part of the Latinos or anyone else. In Nicaragua, we have this problem—not with drugs but with alcohol—and we can't leave anything outside, even though we have nothing of value. People who don't have jobs steal things to maintain their vices or needs. Alcoholics come by and rob us. Sometimes, young people steal wet clothes right off the clothesline.

Her vocabulary, once she left Nicaragua, became more colorful, varied, and more influenced by English and Mexican Spanish. The word "immigration" became *la migra* for the first time when Yamileth was at the Guatemalan-Mexican border. It reversed to *inmigración* throughout Mexico, but, once in the United States, it became *la migra* forever. The word *híjole* also worked its way into Yamileth's speech soon after she arrived in Los Angeles. At the end of January 1989, when she told me about the train trip, I heard her use it for the first time, and now it has become one of her favorite words. The Spanish word *almuerzo* was replaced by the English "lunch," and many other words went through the same transformation.

Although Yamileth made the move to the United States, a centuries-old Nicaraguan tradition, which had originated in Spain, stayed with her: *¿El qué dirán?*, or What will people say? In Nicaragua you heard it in the gossip, the curiosity about each other's homes, including the smallest detail, such as whether a neighbor had salt or not. Neighbors were always there to help, but they would watch comings and goings carefully and be the first to speculate, raising their eyebrows at the visit of a person of the opposite sex. Even the glimpse of a purchase would make them wonder where the money had come from. When a woman's parents die, according to Yamileth, the talk starts. When her mother died, people said that she turned to the street to survive. People in Yamileth's neighborhood had always lived in poverty; a woman living alone couldn't change that, not honorably, anyhow. If anyone had seen her with David, that would have set the neighborhood to clucking and would have compromised her role as a representative of a mass organization of women. She had to know whom to trust but, as always, that involved risks.

Even in her absence, ¿el qué dirán? spun around her. She knew that many Estelianos surmised that Omar's drinking and depression were more severe as a result of her being gone, but it was almost as if the questioning and curious eyes of her Estelí neighbors followed her to Los Angeles. What if they had seen men hassling her on the street? "I almost died of shame one day. I stopped at a corner, and a man who was parked there motioned for me to get in his car. I got right out of there. People could have seen me and thought I was thinking about going with him. It humiliated me so! Now I worry that when someone invites me for a walk, someone I know will think I'm doing that kind of work." Even during the riots, when she saw students running with looted liquor, it bothered her that they were seen on television. What would they have said back in Nicaragua if her family had been seen on television doing something criminal?

"Saving face" seemed to be a preoccupation of Yamileth's and often, in my eyes, an exaggerated sense of one's place. I have seen both Yamileth and Miguel sit at a table and not eat because they believed that they had not done enough work to warrant anyone's feeding them. The thought of seeing Penny after Yamileth had mistakenly told her that Leticia had a job for her made her cry, so she saved face by not going back to Oregon. It is all tied in with ¿el qué dirán? and pride in oneself, but it also may have had as much to do with culture shock and missing her family. In Los Angeles and in the house with her relatives, some version of life as it had been in Nicaragua continued, albeit in an altered state.

The reader may wonder why in Latin America, so exalted for its commitment to family unity, many Nicaraguan women rear their children without the participation of fathers. Early in my research, while talking with the mixture of journalists and adventurers in the bar at the Intercontinental Hotel in Managua, I heard that Nicaragua had always been a country of strong women without men; the years of violence and the irresponsibility of machismo had taken their toll. Nicaraguan women, they said, carried not only the responsibilities of parenting and domestic work but also most of the economic maintenance of the family, to a greater extent than women in other Central American countries. It has been that way for years. Throughout the 1980s, Yamileth talked with me of the naïveté of women who allowed themselves to become single parents, yet that is precisely what happened to her. She told my students that she became pregnant with Diana because, during her brief stay in

Nicaragua, she had had the opportunity to have sex and took advantage of it. The whole class laughed.

Although Yamileth talked about bringing up children being more difficult without a father, she later noted, in response to a question a student of mine asked, that she had never known her own, nor had many Nicaraguans, and that the lack of one had not mattered much in her life or in her children's. She added, however, that it would have been nice to have had one as a role model, but she had done all right anyway. Then she wondered aloud if fathers were more important to people who were used to having them.

In spite of the years that Yamileth spent talking with women about improving their lot in society, she fell into the traps she warned them about, especially when it came to her relationship with David. She could pull back and look objectively at her decisions related to him, but then she would quickly move to the more personal viewpoint, how it looked from her heart. While she clearly identified her relationship with David as one that did not exemplify what she had urged women to create for themselves in Nicaragua, she described only herself as the one "being a little at fault," never mentioning David's responsibility, and in the end worried only about what his wife might think.

She also struggled with her subservient attitude toward Uncle Mundo. Only when Sofía flared up at him in Mexico City did Yamileth finally see the fear in him and shake herself free. When she later threatened to turn him in, she was not the first in the family to do so. Sergio, in an angry discussion with Leticia, had earlier made the same threat. And Yamileth, who was so shy in Mexico that she would have preferred watching television to attending Christmas dinner, who was embarrassed to eat with Penny and Mark on her day off, and who had been afraid to jaywalk, had finally stood up to Uncle Mundo. She could look him in the eye, tell him no, and then threaten him. He was nothing more to her than her sister's husband's brother, and she did not have much use for him. Therefore, telling him no did not bring with it the possibility of losing someone she loved.

Saying no to Miguel would have been entirely different. Yamileth fiercely sheltered him, yet she realized that by keeping Miguel so close to her and by protecting him from the kinds of problems that she had faced, she had limited his ability to take responsibility for himself. As much as she tried to control her own behavior—and I have heard her exhort others in the family to let him take the consequences for his actions—it was difficult to stop and hard to find the balance.

When Yamileth talked about her mother's death, she always cried, but she stopped if Miguel came into the room. As she told of her being in Mexico on the anniversary of her mother's death, she wept, and, as she tried to hide her tears from her son, she explained: "I don't like him to see me crying because it bothers him. It's always better if I hide things." In Estelí, Yamileth and her mother kept their emotions and family tragedies from Miguel. He was never forewarned of Yamileth's dangerous trips to the north. During my visits, I often saw her hurriedly get in an army jeep that had pulled up to their house in Estelí. As she raced out the door, he screamed and cried at the suddenness of her departure, yet they all had spent hours beforehand concealing it from him. I had to bite my tongue.

Obviously, there were times when I thought that I knew better about how things should go in her family, and there were also instances when she thought the same about mine. The day after we learned about my cancer, Yamileth tiptoed up the stairs to my bedroom. "Why," she wondered, "haven't the neighbors come over?" I told her that they didn't know yet. "Where are your friends?" They've been told, I said, but they all work and, really, there's nothing for them to do, at least not now. "Why doesn't your family come to help?" Well, my mother was coming from South Dakota, and my brother Doug would drive her down from the Portland airport. My other brother, Greg, lived in Colorado. Two of our daughters were in college: Lisa in California, and Heather in Pennsylvania. All were far away; there was nothing to be done at this point. Yamileth nodded just to keep me happy.

For years I had shaken my head in dismay as I watched Yamileth and her family make major decisions based on small personal, and at times seemingly overstated, problems within the family. This time, I carefully explained to her, with the hope that someday she would apply this to her own life, that my brothers had good jobs, and that if they were to quit them in the Nicaraguan-López style to rush to my side, then we would really have problems.

"Still," she said, "the cultures are so different," and so were Yamileth and I. In Nicaragua, people would have gathered around my bed, crying, praying, offering to help. "Here," she said, "it is so cold." I knew what she meant, but I was having a hard time trying to figure out a way to deal with cancer and my changed life. A Nicaraguan grieving scene would have frightened me to death before

the cancer killed me. So different were our lives, and how much it
showed! We became more convinced of the rightness of our separate cultures and our personal differences. The crisis allowed no
time for dispassionate discussion or understanding.

She was in Lake Oswego as the house filled up with food and
flowers, and she did not meet my mother and brother. Even if she
had, her questions would have remained. She wanted a Nicaraguan
fuss to be made over me, and I did not. Months later, Yamileth and
I talked about the differences in our cultures and in ourselves. I
asked her if she had ever seen anyone who had lived after having
had breast cancer, and she said no. When I came home with the
diagnosis, she thought that I was as good as dead, which meant to
her that she and Miguel were abandoned in the United States. In
our discussion, she never used the word "cancer."

> It surprised me. You don't accept it when it happens to people
> you respect, you love, to people close to you. And I didn't accept
> it [when it happened to you] and thought it was a lie. For ex-
> ample, when they told me that my mother had died, I said, "No,
> it isn't true." I still haven't accepted it and think that when I get
> to Nicaragua, I'll find her there. These things are as if someone
> were playing a joke on me. I know medicine is advanced here,
> but doctors do make mistakes, and I had faith and hoped that
> they were wrong. But that wasn't the case, and it was a terrible
> blow for me. I had to leave for my new job in Lake Oswego right
> away. What worried me was that I was going to be alone. We're
> not used to that. For us, it's harder because we live so close to-
> gether and get so emotionally involved with each other. If a per-
> son is sick, we're not just going to let them die. You needed
> someone to take care of you and not fall apart on you. So I won-
> dered, "How could Megan possibly be left alone to take care of
> you?"[1] These things made no sense to me.
>
> Miguel asked, "Why don't we tell her that we're going to
> stay to help? That way she won't have to get out of bed." But I
> didn't know what you wanted and thought it was better to say
> nothing. Miguel was afraid. We had just gone through the prob-
> lem with my mother, but in her case we knew it would happen
> gradually. In Nicaragua, people who have your sickness die rap-
> idly. It can happen at any moment. That's the way Miguel saw it.

---

[1]Actually, my husband was home as well as my daughter. Yamileth might
have thought that he would be too busy to be of help, but most likely it was the
way she usually described being alone, as in "I was all alone, all alone, with only
Miguel and my mother."

For example, at every little noise that came out of your room, he'd worry: "What could that be? What can be happening to Diana? Could it be that she's sick? Why don't we go up and see what happened? Why don't you tell her that you'll stay with her?" And when you were alone in your bedroom, he'd say, "If you want, I'll sit near the steps and if she wants something I can call you right away." So he sat on the steps, to see if he could help. For me, it was confusing to see everything going along as it always had, Tomás working and Megan going to classes. It was hard for me to understand.

I reminded her that we like our privacy. Besides, as much as we liked our neighbors, they were not our best friends. I added that we explained the situation to our friends and family on the telephone and that we had invited a small group to come over on the very day that she left. She talked about how those were our customs, but how surprising it had been for her: "When we love, we love to show it, not only by doing things for someone but by solving their problems as if we had supernatural powers and could say I'm going to do this or that. In the culture of my country, sometimes people come out of curiosity and they gossip, but others make these visits from their hearts. But they'd always bring food, a grilled chicken, something to eat, always." I told her that we received enough food for the year and flowers for months, but she remained unconvinced that my culture had any similarities to hers. Even I had to chuckle as I imagined what she would say if she had seen many of the flowers arrive in florists' vans rather than being delivered personally.

It was more than just our cultures that were at odds. We, as very different women, disagreed, and it may have as much to do with social class as anything else. In that situation, Yamileth was dependent upon us, and my sickness was a threat to her well-being. "Miguel was afraid you were going to die, and then what would we do? It was as if both you and Tomás were going to be gone, and he'd have no one to hold on to. He's not used to sicknesses such as yours. We hear of these things but not often. When this happens in Nicaragua, people don't talk about it much, or maybe it hasn't happened to anyone we're close to. Anyhow, we hadn't heard much about it." I told her that I hadn't either, until I got it. We both laughed.

Later that year, in the fall of 1989, Yamileth talked about Lisa's being out of college, Heather's upcoming graduation, and Megan's having started college. Much later, Yamileth and her nieces—especially Marisa—developed a close friendship based on mutual respect and affection, but during their first year in the United States,

Marisa and Sofía had disappointed Yamileth by not attending high
school.[2]

> I like seeing Lisa, so young, and already working. She's respon-
> sible for herself and her things. She feels secure, so to a certain
> point you can rest. She's decided on a career, she'll pay for her-
> self, choose what she wants to choose, and you don't have to
> worry anymore. I look at Leticia and her children who don't know
> anything and don't know what they want. It's a different culture.
> Leticia has to support them and fulfill their every little desire.
> They don't know that they have to learn to do something in order
> to support themselves. I love to see young people in universi-
> ties—Heather, almost done, and Megan, already there. Miguel
> said to his cousins, "Imagine, Sofía, Megan is your age, and she's
> in the university already." But they don't think about the future,
> the present, nothing. None of that exists for them, only the mo-
> ment to eat, to live, and to dance. I went all over Nicaragua talk-
> ing about the rights women should have, but my own nieces aren't
> interested. They think that since they're in the United States, a
> Prince Charming will give them everything they desire. The
> prince, though, is only a story, a legend made for children, and
> he doesn't exist.
>
> The reality is that we're worried more about our work than
> we are about studying. I speak in the name of other Nicaraguans,
> who, through the Revolution, realize that education is what's
> important. The Somoza government didn't teach us the impor-
> tance of education. Latinos from most Central American coun-
> tries have had the same unfortunate experience of living under
> governments that wanted to keep them numb, asleep rather than
> educated. If we were better educated, we'd want to make more
> money, and we'd make more demands. The countries haven't
> wanted that. All of our lives we've worked like *burros* to eat our
> daily bread. Food for each day has been our major worry. Ask
> anyone. We never say, "I'm going to get a job so I can keep on
> studying." No! Almost no one would.

Her nieces were examples of how their culture played out in
the United States, according to Yamileth. They liked hanging out

---

[2]A Rand Corporation study discovered that newly arrived Latinos from the
ages of fifteen to seventeen are less likely than immigrants of that age group
from other countries to attend high school. Instead of starting school, they seek
jobs to help resolve their economic needs. "A Hunger for Education," *Los Angeles Times*, July 15, 1996. Latinos are the immigrants who arrive with the least
amount of academic preparation. "Inmigrantes latinos sufren de disparidad," *La
Opinión*, July 3, 1996.

with boys more than they liked to study. She said that they had become lazy, distracted by the present rather than looking toward the future. Only her niece Marisa, who worked from eight o'clock in the morning until late at night, was spared from harsh criticism. Marisa had to work because she "had assumed the financial responsibility of a parent."

She found it difficult to accept the fact that her nieces and son lacked interest in their own futures because Yamileth had always looked for something more to live for than the day-to-day routine, which is probably one reason why the Nicaraguan Revolution appealed to her and why a humdrum job in the United States did not. "I spent a lot of time working without being paid, out of conviction or I don't know what, and that's good, up to a certain point. You work all the time and then enjoy the fruits of your work. That's what I think is good. People feel proud to have done that."

The differences in cultures cut both ways in her perception. Our children's independence indicated that many of us in the United States are "not so closely tied to the family." Yamileth said, "I like it but don't think I could do it." Her mother always complained about the children's not visiting enough, and she particularly griped about Omar's absence, even though, according to Nicaraguan tradition (as explained to me by the family), a male was supposed to be more attached to his wife than to his mother. Tradition be damned, according to Doña María; Omar was the joy of her life. Happiness was when he walked in, dirty and muddy from work, and hugged her. Yamileth explained it:

> As mother and protector of her children, she had the right to see us all the time. She felt abandoned if two weeks or a month went by and the others hadn't come to see her. She always used the example of my sister Nilda, in Managua, who made an effort to visit and bring her some little thing, soap or cheese. My mother liked that sort of affection. But Leticia, who lived two blocks away, didn't visit unless my mother asked her to, and my mother complained about that. She was jealous of everything, jealous that a child might be with someone else, that a child could be affectionate with someone besides her. She used to say to me, "You can find lots of men, but these men leave and die, and you'll still be here. But you're not going to have another mother." And that's true.

I asked why the family members had so many economic ties among themselves and why there seemed to be little financial independence. It was difficult for her to answer; and, when she did, she focused on Omar and how he has had opportunities different from hers, therefore making her responsible for him and, by extension, for anything that happened to her family in Nicaragua. Family members encouraged the ensuing guilt, and so did neighbors. Lives were so tightly linked that the family's economic and emotional tug-of-war always targeted one of its members. If one momentarily came into some money, and another needed it, the money went to help the needy one. In such an arrangement, no one was ever allowed to become rich or drastically poorer than another. Their links served as a financial leveler and as a guarantee of their well-being. To complete the circle, the shared poverty reenforced the economic ties.

A discussion of family always returned to money and food, as happens in many shared living situations. Their lifelong struggle for beans and rice had made every little portion of food or can of soda valuable. Eating was not something they took for granted, and they showed their generosity and concern for each other by assuring themselves that everyone had eaten. Yet, at the same time, the amount one consumed was carefully watched by everyone in the house. If you did not work for the food, it was not right to eat it. Outrage was directed toward any freeloader or perceived scrounger. The criticism was returned by an anger that eventually found a more obvious leech on the family's resources, as happened when the family criticized Yamileth and she turned on Leticia's boyfriend and called him a parasite. The spiral, set up years ago, continued to spin.

When she said that she had told the school principal "some truth and some lies" to embellish their dire financial situation so that the children would be fed at school, it was so close to the truth that I questioned whether Yamileth had lied at all. Food and the quest for it, always of primary concern in Nicaragua, remained high in Los Angeles, and she wondered why more people did not steal food during the Los Angeles riots. In an editorial in the *Los Angeles Times*, the writer said that "some whites called the riots a crime spree. Some blacks called it a political uprising. For the Latinos who took part, it was a bread riot."[3]

Later, Yamileth talked about the U.S. work ethic. She expected people to work hard, but it also frightened her. She was not sure that she wanted to pay the price, which she saw as it being more

[3]"L.A.'s Unfinished Business," *Los Angeles Times*, April 28, 1995.

difficult to spend time with her children in the United States than it had been in Nicaragua. Doña María was no longer alive to fill in for her. Her attitude changed somewhat when work became synonymous with the bakery. As always, Yamileth had a goal different from just making money. She wanted to create a future, something they all would have together. The bakery offered that possibility, and she would have worked twenty-four hours a day had her body allowed it. Nonetheless, she worried about the hours spent. "If you work that hard, you never see your children. You don't know what they're thinking. Then the gangs in the school take advantage of that to attract children. Where we live, the schools are dangerous, with problems from the fifth grade on. Even though parents don't want their children to be gang members, children see their friends at school more than they see their parents, and those friends have more influence on them." The idea of working for a goal appealed to her:

> When people from the United States visited Nicaragua, I knew that they had saved money for their vacation and that they spent it learning about Nicaragua. But I never imagined that people worked so hard. It was a big surprise. In Nicaragua we work and save, but never to visit another place. We've never had the chance, but here people do. I love that. For example, if I wanted to work hard here, make some money, and give myself a good party for my birthday—the kind of party I've never had—I'd do it and be happy with it. I like it that people here can work, save their money, and do whatever they want.

Acutely seeing herself as a role model, she taught her children and nieces by her example. At their urging, Yamileth told me the cantina story as soon as I had reached my Los Angeles hotel in 1989. Excitement and disgust crowded the room as her relatives added to her account or reminded her of forgotten elements. They all loved to see my eyes widen in horror as the story progressed. (Later, I asked her to retell it for my tape recorder, but she could not muster up the drama of that first time.) Yamileth had once worked in Nicaragua to rehabilitate prostitutes, so she had some understanding of the women's plight. After relating her experience, she added that she thought "that 70 or 80 percent of the women in the cantina were waiting for a Prince Charming to take them out of there with the dream of having children together and being provided a clean life. As far as I'm concerned, the idea of a woman finding a place of dignity never dies."

Changes in Our Relationship

The first year that they were in the United States was a time of
great change for all of us. Although Yamileth had met my husband
several times in Nicaragua, she knew little about my personal life.
With her 1989 visit to our home, the professional perspective that I
had maintained—and perhaps that was there on her part, too—began to disappear, and our differences became more apparent than
they ever had been in Nicaragua. Toward the end of the year, I
realized that Yamileth and her family were becoming Nicaraguan
Americans, whether they wanted to or not, and for the first time I
found our cultural differences troubling. In Estelí, as I listened to
their struggle against the Somozas, to their defiance of the Contras,
and to all that they lost in their hope to be free, I saw them as admi-
rable, even virtuous, given the disadvantages of their lives and the
goals that they had. Their roles were modest and down-to-earth,
but they and thousands like them overthrew a dictator and his hench-
men. Some cheered them on, and some fought against them. Nicaragua, a small, spirited country, had the attention of the world.

Their transition to living in the United States was awkward for
me. On the one hand, had they stayed in Nicaragua, I would have
seen their revolutionary dream burn out even further. On the other
hand, watching them adapt to the U.S. culture caused an emotional
and intellectual argument within me. While they imitated the culture of the industrialized world and, in particular, that of Southern
California, it seemed to me that they often imitated the worst parts
of it.

That first year, as I watched the news on television and saw
Panamanians loot stores and Eastern Europeans flock across their
borders to shop, it became apparent that the freedom to acquire
was on its way to becoming a universal goal. The lures of materialism and consumerism could not be resisted, and technology held
out the promise of equalizing people and countries. Ideologies did
not count anymore; VCRs did. As Yamileth said, her fondest desire
was to own a VCR, and when she had the opportunity to buy one,
she did.

As someone pointed out, I have three television sets in my
house; why would I not expect the Nicaraguans to want the same?
I questioned such an expense when people were on the edge of
financial chaos, which is where the family usually was. And I questioned their use of television. They thought that it stimulated their
children's imaginations, and I thought that it stunted them. Just

because they were in the United States and bought the same set, I expected them to use it the same way that I did. We agreed that television should be used educationally, but their concept of its role in their children's education was different from mine. They wanted their children to watch Mexican soap operas, while I urged programs in English. It was unfair of me. I had imposed my own expectations on them. I called a friend of mine, Cyd Perhats, best described as a Chicago Oregonian, who had once been with me in Nicaragua. She commented that I was painfully watching with the eyes of our culture as it was mirrored by the Nicaraguans, and she was right. The Nicaraguans, in their imitation of us, made me see more clearly what I did not like about my own culture. It was not theirs that I had problems with; it was mine.

One night in Los Angeles, I invited the family to have dinner in a Nicaraguan restaurant. Sofía's Central American boyfriend came along, and during the meal he mentioned how much he liked Rambo movies, the Reagan-era Commie-bashing ones. I said that I had often thought that Rambo represented the United States in its relations with developing nations. We controlled and destroyed countries, Central American ones among them, under the guise of eliminating Communists, who in those days were spotted everywhere south of the border. The family, however, saw Rambo as a good example for children. He represented someone doing good for his government by conquering evil. I suppose that they could even relate it to the Sandinistas' struggle to rid themselves of the Contras. I was stunned that one of the shallowest examples of the macho tough guy and the U.S. attitude that typified the 1980s had become someone to be admired by citizens of the same countries bullied by perpetrators of the Rambo mindset.

Then again, why would I expect them to see a relationship between Rambo and Central America? Why would I expect them to see the role of the U.S. government from my point of view? Because I had learned so much about their lives after years of interviewing, I imagined that they knew as much about mine. But they did not. I was the student of their lives; they were not students of mine. And even if they had known what I thought, there was no reason for them to agree with me. That was eight years ago. Today, there are two television sets in their small apartment. Television, however, has lost some of its charm for Yamileth, and she worries about Miguel and Nora: "They're stuck to the television set. They like soap operas. That's not good because they don't like to read, and if they do read, they don't know what they've read. They're not centered on what they're doing. Instead, they're listening to television or what's going on in the house."

Nonetheless, they are all learning to speak English—some more than others[4]—and I do my part by giving them books at every opportunity. Yamileth encourages them to read and admonishes Nora and Miguel when they avoid it. "Even if you read and don't go to school, books help you to see more. What a beautiful thing it is to read important things! I love it. I tell Nora that if she reads a fantastic story and really pays attention to it, she'll begin to see the countryside and what goes on there. But neither one of them does it. When they watch television and someone else is talking, they don't hear him or see him. You have to touch them and say *shu, shu* to wake them up."

So there we are: Yamileth sounds more like me, and I no longer pass judgment, or question purchases or decisions; and they, too, have become independent from my opinions. The friendship, however, is lopsided, as it must be given the condition under which it began and flourished. I might know more about Yamileth than any other American does, but even though the physical and emotional space between us has diminished, she still does not know nearly as much about me. I have not gone to her for advice, but she comes to me. She talks; I listen. That is how it started out, and that is how it will always be. The pattern, like that of many families, was established long ago.

---

[4]Yamileth understands English but rarely speaks it, at least not in front of me.

Ten

The Changing Face of Los Angeles

Yamileth left Nicaragua, a country at war, and moved to the United States only to find herself in another war that raged in the streets of South-Central Los Angeles. There was no way for her to anticipate the role that the police, the gangs, an African American named Rodney King, the economy, the schools, *la migra*, and Proposition 187 would play in her future. She arrived the same decade that tens of thousands of other Central Americans did, causing a huge influx that pushed Los Angeles's Latino population to more than 40 percent of the total inhabitants of the city. Some called it *la reconquista*, the reconquest of land that the United States had taken by force more than 140 years ago. The city's old-timers—unless they managed to isolate themselves in Westside enclaves—would testify that nearly everywhere they went, someone spoke Spanish, although Yamileth's first days seemed to her to be a nightmarish blur of English.[1]

As the demographics changed, so did employment opportunities. The city's service sector hired fewer African Americans and more Latinos. Undocumented Latinos such as the Lópezes often accepted wages and conditions that many African Americans, as citizens, would not tolerate. Even legal immigrants were slow to complain about job inequities. Moreover, most recently arrived Latinos were deferential, a characteristic attractive to employers. Whatever the case, in the faltering economy of Los Angeles, jobs were scarce for everyone; and when Yamileth lost her bakery, she was not alone. Hard times in Southern California especially struck minority businesses, of which Los Angeles County had the highest

---

[1]Once I stayed in a hotel near downtown Los Angeles for ten days and spoke English only once, and that was when I happened to have a taxi driver from Russia.

concentration in the United States. As the number of frustrated job seekers increased, so did the number on welfare. To many Californians, the large influx of legal and illegal immigrants worsened the economy and caused many of the skyrocketing welfare expenses. Often obscured in the debate was the fact that only the children born in the United States are eligible for general welfare; their undocumented parents are not. The argument heated up, and one target was the number of immigrants using maternity and pediatric services. In Los Angeles County, children—among them Diana— born to undocumented immigrants accounted for more than 65 percent of all births at county-run hospitals.

One November day in 1991, while Yamileth was pregnant and I was there to interview her, she said that she had a medical appointment that would take her all day. All day? Because that seemed impossible to me, I decided to go along. Marisa dropped us off at eight o'clock in the morning at the H. Claude Hudson Comprehensive Health Care Center and the County Department of Public Social Services next door. By nine o'clock, Yamileth had accomplished quite a bit: she found out that she did not have tuberculosis, paid thirty dollars for her last checkup, and received an unexpected appointment with WIC (Women, Infants, and Children Program). She had never heard of WIC and had never asked for an appointment, but, as I watched, someone wordlessly handed her the appointment slip.[2] So far, so good. Things had moved quickly. I told Yamileth that whatever lay ahead of us, it would not take all day. She just smiled.

We checked into the Department of Public Social Services at one minute past nine o'clock. All Yamileth wanted was to be told what hospital she should go to when she went into labor. It reached ninety-one degrees in Los Angeles that day. The rooms were not air-conditioned, and soon all the smoke in the "No Smoking" room stung my eyes. A large fan tried to circulate the stale air. We waited. At ten o'clock, a series of recalls began, which meant that the one hundred fifty or so people in the room had to line up again and put their names on a list. That took an hour to do. Because the computer age had not yet reached the Los Angeles Department of Public Social Services, everyone's name went on a piece of paper that simply stayed on the table until the next recall an hour or so later, when it was replaced by another piece of paper.

---

[2]She kept the appointment, but, because she was in the United States illegally, she was not eligible for benefits.

I left at noon. Yamileth got home at four o'clock. She had been told, late in the afternoon, that her social worker was not even there that day, so Yamileth could not be seen. She was resigned, used to the experience; I was furious. Six days later, most of the staff at Public Social Services walked out on a one-day strike. A little over a month later, the Hudson Center, the county's largest public clinic, had to turn away about thirty patients per day, adding them to a waiting list that included eight hundred women. Bad as the situation had seemed to me, it had gotten worse; and it turned out that, a few years before, it had been worse still—people had been known to have their babies before they could get a prenatal appointment.[3]

Yamileth delivered her baby at Los Angeles County-USC Medical Center, which operates the largest emergency department in the nation. Stories abounded in the newspaper about the crowded hospital and long waiting periods. Nonetheless, that was not her experience, as she describes in her testimony.

The immigration debate swirled around them, with most of the complaints directed toward Latinos, the largest group. While many Angelenos argued that immigrants should not bear the responsibility for Los Angeles's woes, others addressed their own alienation from the city and the ensuing conflict of cultures. Letters to newspapers complained about shoot-outs, barbaric gangs, primitive youth, hardened police, bankrupt schools, overburdened welfare and public housing programs, crowded and lawless county hospitals, and waves of immigrants running down the freeways. Many blamed the rise in the numbers of undocumented immigrants for the change in a city that, until a few decades ago, had been white and Protestant. African Americans, too, had their complaints, addressed when one wrote that in his neighborhood, which was near Yamileth's, "Latinos put twenty to thirty people in a home, kept goats, grew corn in the front yard, and hung their wash on the front fence." He added, "It's a culture clash."[4] The clash also existed within the Latino community itself: 75 percent of Mexican Americans thought that too many immigrants had arrived, and three-quarters of California's Latinos viewed undocumented

[3]Claire Spiegel, "Clinic Shuts Out Patients Seeking Prenatal Care," *Los Angeles Times,* December 12, 1991.

[4]Terry Anderson, "The Culture Clash in South-Central L.A.," *Los Angeles Times*, May 29, 1996.

immigration as a problem.[5] Even Yamileth admitted that Los Angeles had probably been a cleaner and less dangerous place before all of the Latinos arrived.

Others argued that Latinos had greatly contributed to the cultural and economic life of California. Compared to other ethnic groups, Latinos, as typified by the López family, worked harder, maintained stronger family ties and values, had fewer illnesses, and had a high employment rate, albeit in low-paid positions. Some studies suggested that immigrants—both legal and illegal—contributed more to California in taxes than they cost in government services, but there was no doubt that a wage gap persisted. "For immigrants from Central America and Mexico, average wages were 25 percent to 40 percent lower than natives in 1970; by 1990 the difference had grown to 50 percent."[6]

Many Californians assumed that all immigrants had false documents. The Lópezes initially considered the buying of false papers as dishonest. As I walked through Pico-Union one day with Yamileth, vendors hawking false papers crowded the corners. At that time, however, she was reluctant to buy them. The tradition of worrying about what people will say was alive and well for some in Pico-Union and South-Central Los Angeles, just as it was in the small Nicaraguan city that the Lópezes came from.

In general, Yamileth and her family were more likely than non-Latinos to be the victims of violence, household crimes, and fraud. A federal report indicated that the Latino rate of robberies and aggravated assaults was higher than for the non-Latino. And, as in the family's case, much of the Latino population was relatively young, poor, and concentrated in urban neighborhoods, making them vulnerable to crime. The Lópezes and many other Latinos carried cash. Many did not trust banks, and Yamileth, as an undocumented immigrant, could not get a bank account. Often their money was stolen, as was the case when she was robbed in broad daylight on Olympic Boulevard. And many undocumented immigrants believed—accurately or not—that they could be deported if they contacted the authorities.

With so many gang-related deaths in the county, the murders no longer attracted much media interest unless they reached other

---

[5]Sonia Nazario, "Natives, Newcomers at Odds in East L.A.," ibid., March 4, 1996.

[6]Elaine Wood and Patrick Lee, "Latino Immigrants' Wages, Education Lag, Studies Find," ibid., July 3, 1996.

parts of the city or nonminorities. Attention drawn by gangs focused on African Americans for a long time, although almost twice as many Latinos were killed and significantly more Latinos belonged to gangs. Gradually, young people who had traditionally killed within their own racial or ethnic groups began to target others, turning African-American and Latino gangs against each other.

In Pico-Union, Latino gang members hit the corners by five o'clock every afternoon. The Lópezes knew some of them, and Leticia had even visited one of them in jail. One day, as she was walking down the street, she found herself approaching a gun battle between two opposing gangs. "When they saw me, they recognized me because I had done their hair. They stopped shooting and waved me through. Afterward, they started shooting again." Only a few of the López family adjusted somewhat to the violence, and the worries about the younger members of the family never abated.

The first contact that the younger López children had with gang-related violence began when they started school. There had been nothing in Nicaraguan schools to prepare them for the brutality in Los Angeles. Instead of old-fashioned fistfights, students had gunfights. At the same time, officials called for a cutback of police in the schools. Facing a budget crisis, the Los Angeles Unified School District officials not only had trouble protecting their students, but they also considered shortening the school year, eliminating teaching positions, cutting salaries, and squeezing even more children into already crowded classrooms. Out of desperation, many Angelenos proposed that the system be broken down into smaller districts, while others protested that such a division would be drawn along racial lines. A deadly earthquake severely damaged buildings, and there seemed to be no solution to the overwhelming problems. Not the least of them was the change in demographics: Latinos made up nearly 66 percent of the students. It seemed to have happened suddenly, at least to white Los Angeles, that only 12 percent of the public school population was white. With little left to lose, reform began.

The Riots of 1992

April 29, 1992, started off like any other day in sunny California. Marisa, Manuel, and Nora went shopping that afternoon at the Baldwin Hills Crenshaw Plaza. When they entered the mall around three-thirty, the intersections were quiet; when they came out two hours later, the climate had changed. Unbeknown to them, the

Rodney King verdict was in. African Americans surrounded them, calling them "whites," and chased them to their car.

As Manuel steered his car into the street, an Asian woman stopped hers to allow him to go ahead. When he braked for the red light at the intersection of Crenshaw and Martin Luther King, Jr., Boulevards, angry crowds were beating people whom they had yanked from cars. An African-American man turned the corner, pulled his car up next to Manuel, and warned him to get out of there. The light was still red, but Manuel went through it.

In his rearview mirror, he saw the African-American man maneuver his car to block the lane Manuel had just left. Manuel initially viewed that action as a means of impeding others from chasing him, but he quickly realized that it actually prevented the Asian woman from leaving. In horror, he watched the crowd pull her from her car and pummel her. The family then sped home, running into the house screaming about what had just happened to them. Shades pulled, lights off, they watched the looting and violence on television. In spite of Yamileth's careful meal planning, they were left with only six eggs in the house when the riots began and no food for Diana.

Leticia continued working in her Pico-Union salon, not knowing that a riot had begun. "I saw it later on television but it seemed far away, unimportant, and I certainly didn't think it would become as big as it did. When I called Yamileth to see what was happening, she told me that things weren't good. The following morning, I called again, and they told me they had nothing to eat and couldn't leave because it was dangerous and fires were starting. Nothing had happened where I live, so I took food to them.

"One of my most frightening moments was afterward, when I returned to Jon's Market to look for some beans and some vegetables for myself. At the very moment when I was putting the beans in a bag, everyone inside Jon's began to scream, yelling, 'They're burning the front! Get out! Leave! Let's go!' Everyone began to run, trying to pay at once. I said to Sofía, who had gone with me, 'Let's get out of here.' When we left, they were already burning buildings near us on Alvarado Street and looting the liquor store."

Yamileth remembers that the rest of the family stayed in their South-Central home, hoping that their house looked empty. "We were quiet and made no noise. When it was calm, we went to the corner. Marisa had to wear a scarf because she had dyed her hair blonde. People might think that she was an American and, just for that, beat her and kill her."

From the corner, Yamileth saw television cameras focus on American students running to loot the Sorbonne Plaza, which was burned to the ground by the rioters, "then racing back, hiding their boxes of liquor with a shirt. For us, it was shocking to watch it all on television and then leave and see it ourselves from the corner. Or if we had looted and then had been seen on television, as the students were—*ay*, no! It did seem curious to us why people stole things that weren't food. That's the first thing I'd go after, not a television set, sound equipment, or a chair. I don't understand it, but that's what they took." Everyone in their quiet neighborhood stayed home and hoped for the worst to pass, or so the family thought until a few days later, when six Los Angeles Police Department patrol cars arrived with a police truck. The policemen entered homes and apartments along the street and placed the booty curbside for the truck to pick up.

Not to be stopped by a riot and helped by a *cundina* (an informal banking and lending society among Latinos), the indomitable Leticia opened her own beauty salon in the Pico-Union area just days later, hoping that people would eventually venture out. The whole family pitched in, twelve to thirteen hours per day, seven days per week, just as they had in the bakery. After work, they went to late-night English classes and hoped that no one would shoot them on the perilous trip home. A couple of weeks before the riots, Manuel had found a job with a computer company, now a pile of rubble in Koreatown and dramatic testimony to the family's struggle and hardship. Little money was coming in and their rent was overdue; Yamileth lamented, "It's not like my country where you can say, 'I'll pay you later.'"

They did discuss alternatives, and Marisa said that they considered leaving because "it's so dangerous in Los Angeles that we can no longer put up with the fear." Yamileth agreed. "It's true, you feel tension and pressure in the air. There you are, looking around with your bag tucked under your arm, running at full speed, and at any moment the people around you might rob you of the little food you were able to buy. But as bad as it all is, earthquakes scare me even more."[7]

As a result of the riots after the Rodney King verdict, thousands of jobs were lost, many of them permanently. President George

---

[7]The Managua earthquake of 1972 was not strong in Estelí; nonetheless, the horror of that quake predisposed the López family to have a healthy fear of such a disaster happening again.

Bush came to town and declared the riots a national disaster. He promised help—and rarely mentioned Latinos—but it either took months to arrive or never came at all. The unemployment rate in the area rose, making the poor even poorer. Many of the media framed the riots as an African-American versus white issue, or as a Korean versus African-American one. Although Latino involvement and loss received scant attention, the statistics told a different story: more than 50 percent of those arrested were Latinos, as were one-third of the dead. Some 30 to 40 percent of destroyed businesses were Latino-owned. Half the population in the area affected by the riots was Latino.

Nonetheless, many Angelenos were slow to understand. A reporter, ignorant of the changed demographics in his own city, when asked during the riots where South-Central Los Angeles was, answered that it was wherever reporters found African Americans. Even some Latinos—including Yamileth—did not realize that they made up 50 percent of South-Central Los Angeles and 75 percent of Pico-Union and Koreatown. Most people thought that Latinos lived in East Los Angeles, not in the center of the city. The Latino story was underreported or overlooked, and, even though the media later sought to bring attention to it, the perception remained that South-Central Los Angeles was primarily African-American. To this day, much of the city views the riots through the ethnic and racial demographics of the 1960s, and few seem to notice that Watts now celebrates Cinco de Mayo.

Latinos questioned why their leadership, usually quick to grab the headlines, had been noticeably quiet and slow to react after the riots, pointedly aligning itself with the more established Latino area of East Los Angeles and separating its people from the more recent arrivals from Central America in Pico-Union and South-Central. None of this bode well for the rights of newcomers, documented or not, and illustrated deep divisions in the leadership and in Latino communities. Certainly, all politicians kept in mind voting patterns: although Latinos were 40 percent of the population, they were only 6 percent of the voters.

The role of Latinos in the Los Angeles riots had embarrassed many Latinos, and Yamileth, as quiet as she was about being Nicaraguan and as loyal as she remained to her own country, like all of the family, clearly identified herself as Latino. Just as she had acknowledged the conflicts within the Nicaraguan culture, she recognized the differences within the Latino community in the United States, yet she embraced the commonality of her ethnicity: "We're part of the family. We're all Latinos. It's not my country, but I am still ashamed of what has happened. Those of us who live here have all come with the hope of learning and advancing and not going backward, but what these people did was to go backward instead of going forward. There's no reason to come here to rob. They could have learned that in their own country and not shame the rest of us here. We're representatives, and even though we don't come from the same countries, we're all Latinos."

Although the plight of the Latino community in general received little notice, immigrants did, with the obvious target being the vote-less, unrepresented, and undocumented. The question of what to do about "illegal aliens" popped up on television political advertisements, on the news, and out of the mouths of politicians. A former commissioner of the Immigration and Naturalization Service (INS) urged a "war" against undocumented immigrants by asking that they be denied jobs, education, public housing, and drivers' licenses, and found support from California's Governor Pete Wilson, who kicked off his short-lived presidential campaign by assailing undocumented immigration as he posed in front of the Statue of Liberty. Many Californians desperately hoped that the federal government would come through with funds that had been promised as far back as 1986.

In the fall of 1994, Californians approved Proposition 187 with the intent to deny undocumented immigrants education, social services, and health care. In addition, it required teachers, doctors, and police to report those immigrants to officials. Uncertainty about the measure's status generated anxiety in California's immigrant community, prompting some of its members to forego medical treatment and others to take their children out of school even though the teachers in the Los Angeles Unified School District insisted that their job was to educate, not to serve as Immigration officials. A few weeks later, a federal district court judge blocked major portions of the measure from taking effect until a trial had determined its constitutionality. Proposition 187 is still tied up in the courts.

Immigrants were not alone in their confusion. Some restaurant owners, manufacturers, contractors, hotel and office building owners, and landscapers as well as ranchers and farmers predicted financial disaster. Some economists saw immigration as a net benefit because immigrants pay taxes, use services in moderation, develop thousands of small businesses every year, work in industries that might otherwise move overseas in search of lower-cost labor, and undertake jobs that U.S. workers find undesirable. Others disagreed, arguing that immigrants displace U.S. workers, particularly those with equivalent skills or training, and that immigrant workers depress wages and undermine working conditions. Already disadvantaged minorities were hurt most by the continuing entry of immigrants, who competed with them for scarce low-skilled jobs.

Many of the Californians who voted for Proposition 187 did so out of frustration. It was not just about money, no matter how persistently people framed immigration in that context; it had more to do with the fact that everything had changed, especially in Los Angeles. Polls showed that the most frequently cited reason for voting for the proposition was to send a message to federal and state government officials.

La reconquista? No. Even with large numbers of Latinos in Los Angeles, the newer ones, mostly from Central America, were still relatively unnoticed and unrepresented. For the López family, the riots had reinforced their desire to remain ignored, unarmed, and unharmed. In the city that they described as "getting uglier every day" and that Mayor Richard Riordan called a "war zone," the Lópezes simply wanted to work and to eat their daily food without any attention being called to them. To stay quietly undocumented, they said, continued to be their American dream.

Epilogue

Although I have continued to interview Yamileth, her last lengthy testimony in this text occurred in 1992. A year later, Yamileth's desperation for work led her to ask a niece to help her buy a false green card. It was easy, she later told my students, because you can buy whatever you want in Los Angeles; you just need to get in line. It cost fifty dollars and took her an hour. Amateurish as the card looked, it worked, even to the point that she used it to obtain a valid Social Security number. She found a job, much as immigrants have for over a century, in "light manufacturing"—more aptly described as a sweatshop—sewing the "cone" for bras and shoulder pads. The sweatshop, a day-and-night operation owned and managed by people Yamileth described as Arabs, paid the minimum wage by check and withheld taxes, as required by law.

She eventually earned slightly more than the minimum, but the one hundred sixty dollars she brought home every week amounted to less than the price of one night at a luxury hotel ten miles down the freeway. The owners allowed the workers to go to the bathroom when they wished, but they were certainly discouraged from doing so very often. She considered the work dangerous and showed me marks where the hot equipment had burned her arms. Although the air was bad, no one wore masks, and many of the employees were sick. Yamileth developed an allergy to the fabrics and eventually sought treatment from an allergist who prescribed cortisone. Her coworkers—Nicaraguans, Mexicans, Salvadorans, and Colombians—kept silent about their politics; she shared her political sentiments with one other worker, another Sandinista.

For the first couple of years after Diana's birth, Yamileth occasionally talked with Alejandra in Nicaragua, who kept her informed of David's activities—usually planting or harvesting. When Alejandra saw David, she showed him photographs of the little girl that Yamileth had sent. Yamileth no longer hoped that some day her relationship with her lover would be the same as it once was;

instead, she said, she lived with what she called "the illusion" of being able to return to Nicaragua. However, to imagine taking Diana to a country that seemed besieged by one crisis after another seemed selfish to her. Moreover, she said, milk for her daughter was much too expensive there. Like many who leave with the promise to return, life is lived at the moment. Yamileth was in Los Angeles, and the Revolution and its dreams were long gone.

Even so, Yamileth still considered herself a Sandinista as well as someone capable of doing something useful besides supporting herself and her children. The FSLN leaders asked her to participate in an analysis of the errors they committed, with the hope that it would lead to the understanding of why people left Nicaragua. Through the salon, she met another group of Nicaraguans from a variety of political backgrounds, and they worked together to unite against deportation, not mentioning their differing political viewpoints in the process.

I asked Yamileth about her dream of buying a VCR and how that desire looked to her now. Before I had even gotten the entire question out of my mouth, she started to laugh. She said that at one time a VCR had been like a toy to a poor child who has never had any toys, a fantasy that was impossible in a country where such dreams never came true. Now that she was surrounded by agencies and businesses that would allow her to buy anything she wanted on credit, she no longer had those desires. She had, she said, "a purse full of plastic." Although a bank offered her five thousand dollars worth of credit without "knowing" her, her legal situation prevented her from being able to obtain a checking or savings account. Besides, she had a VCR; and, as she put it, "material things never really interested me." She had learned, as many of us have, that it is easier to disdain materialism from a relatively comfortable position than it is from an absolutely untenable one.

In 1996 she married Eddie, born in the United States to Latino parents. She liked Eddie but mainly saw him as her chance to eventually get her hands on a legal work permit. He also liked Yamileth, but somehow had formed the idea that anyone who owned a house in Nicaragua must have some money. When he asked her, "When you die, who will inherit your house?" she enigmatically answered, "What I have is yours." She and I both laughed at his ignorance of her country, and she wondered aloud why anyone would think she worked in a sweatshop if she had money. She kept him away from her apartment and the bed she shared with the children, meeting him almost clandestinely, as had been her custom in Nicaragua, but without the deep affection she had felt for David. She thought that if she obtained legal papers, she might be able to visit Nicaragua one day.

Miguel

In August 1993, Miguel flew to Portland, Oregon, where Ken, Mark, and Penny waited for him. A week earlier, when Mark and Penny had called inviting him to visit, Miguel's answer was an immediate yes. When they asked Yamileth if he could stay in Oregon to go to school, the answer was again yes, but was not quite so quick or enthusiastic. Miguel had quit his Los Angeles high school, and concerns were high that he would be left with no real skills. Mark and Penny had already talked with his former teacher and had investigated soccer and baseball teams for him to join. He would start high school in Lake Oswego and have another chance. After two weeks, however, Miguel decided to return to Los Angeles—he missed his family too much to live away from them—and he ended up promising all of us to complete high school there.

For me, Miguel's trip to Oregon marked a significant change. We were not able to see him, but he and I had a few arguments on the telephone. I thought he should stay; he disagreed. The Miguel of four years ago was long gone. Yamileth may have mothered him too much, as she would say, but the young man on the other end of the phone was able to stand up to me, argue with me, disagree with me. I, as any proud parent, was mostly happy that he could do so. He was no longer a child, and when he promised to go back to high school, I believed him. He had earlier joined a youth group at Blessed Sacrament Church in the Hollywood area, and the leaders had been encouraging him to speak up and take charge of his life. Going to high school was part of it.

When he returned, he began to question the existence of God, leaving Yamileth without answers. He started a new high school, Manual Arts, but he occasionally skipped classes, complaining of recurring headaches; at other times, he stayed home for no reason that Yamileth could discern. When she questioned him, he "raised his voice" to her, something that she had never thought that he would do. She responded by limiting his freedom—making him stay home from social events put on by the youth group—and by explaining her version of cooperation to him: "You give to me, I give to you. But if you don't, then nothing." Life with a small child and an adolescent boy was stressful, or, as she described it, "complicated with

lots of problems," especially for someone who finds it so difficult
to say no to those she loves.

Although money was a problem, nearly everyone who worked—
and that was everyone who was not in school—had a car. Miguel
was stopped by the police in 1995 for running a red light in
Yamileth's car and for not having a driver's license. The car was
impounded for a month and he was fined; the whole experience
cost him a thousand dollars but the family was grateful that when
the police took away his false green card, they did not deport him.
Nonetheless, he had to come up with the money, which required
him to stop attending the few eleventh-grade classes he did go to
and instead work full-time with his mother in the sweatshop.

Miguel started lifting weights, and the small child with all the
intestinal parasites became a muscular young man as he reached
his twenties, looking much like his father Antonio, who died in
1979. He still belongs to his church group, and among the members are at least two girlfriends. When he goes out in the evening,
Yamileth prefers that he go with his church group or with other
Nicaraguans to sites outside of South-Central Los Angeles and Pico-
Union. If he arrives home late, she lies awake worrying that the
gangs have grabbed him. He gives her his paycheck every week,
and, in turn, she hands him twenty dollars. God must love her, she
said, to give her such a good son.

Diana

By the time Diana was two years of age, she had taken over the
house. If Yamileth criticized her, then the rest of the family admon-
ished Yamileth, who longed to but was unable to administer the
stern discipline advocated by her own mother. By the age of three
and one-half, the birth of other children had changed the family
dynamics and Diana no longer had control. One day I watched her,
dressed in baby blue and striking a pose whenever my hand neared
my camera, as she walked over to the VCR—the toy of her mother's
fantasy—pushed some buttons, removed the tape, and replaced it
with another one more to her liking. By four, she began calling her
mother "Mom" in English; and once, when Yamileth mentioned
that an actor on television was good-looking, the little girl turned
away from the television set and said, "Not for you." Obviously,
she still thought that she retained some power in the household.
Leticia and her daughters long ago stopped asking Yamileth for the
name of Diana's father and she has not told them. Diana, however,

does ask. Yamileth replies by saying that he is far away and changes the subject. She has no idea how she will answer as Diana becomes older and her questions more persistent.

Leticia

Missing from the family setting is Leticia's husband. After the 1990 elections in Nicaragua, Sergio went back to Estelí where he started his life over with a new wife and began another family. He returned to Los Angeles once and saw his first grandchild, but he has yet to see his second. Uncle Mundo, too, moved back to Nicaragua and no longer works as a *coyote*. Leticia eventually kicked out the Salvadoran boyfriend and then took up with a singer who later returned to Mexico. The beauty salon that she opened in Pico-Union supported the family, most of whom worked there at one time or another. Leticia's success led her to expand, adding experts in weight control and more space. Her shop has become the center of the neighborhood where everyone congregates to gossip, have fun, and play with the children. Nonetheless, the tensions of living in Los Angeles have kept her ever vigilant and open to options in other cities and even other countries. Somewhere, life must be better than where she has lived. And maybe Nora could attend a university if, as Letitia said, they moved to Mexico.

Marisa and Manuel

Soon after the riots, at the Los Angeles home of my good friends Bob and Kitty Shepard, I met their friend John Gilmore, whom they called Big John. After a spirited discussion about politics, work ethics, and immigration, Big John said that he would call Manuel—who by then was a legal resident—and offer him a job in his warehouse. He did so, and Manuel accepted. Later, Marisa, laughing with joy, said that one thing they had learned was that whether you are in the United States, Mexico, or Nicaragua, it is whom you know that counts. I could only agree.

Marisa and Manuel had their first child in early 1994, Stephanie María—a name difficult for Yamileth to pronounce because in Spanish, when the letter "s" is followed by a consonant, it is preceded by an "e," making the Spanish version Estefanía. Marisa laughed and said, "We gave her a very American name!" I doubt that the symbolism was missed by any of us.

Sofía, Chela, and Nora

Sofía married a Mexican who is a legal resident and gave birth to a son a year later. A year or so after Chela graduated from high school, she married a non-Spanish-speaking American. Nora graduated from Woodland Hills Middle School's bilingual program, continued with high school, and counted Chinese and Armenian students among her friends.

Omar

In Estelí, Omar and Irene stayed in Yamileth's duplex with their children. Irene washed and ironed clothes, as Omar's mother had done for years, and occasionally worked at a child-care center. Omar had no job—the unemployment rate was estimated to be between 65 and 75 percent—but he sometimes found work in construction. His conversion to the Mormon religion gave him temporary relief from his drinking. For the first time in Estelí, there were street children sniffing glue, abandoned by parents who could no longer take care of them. The schools had become private. Omar could not afford to send his young children on a regular basis, but he managed to keep them off the streets.[1] A teenage son, Daniel, joined the military, while another, Noel, served as a Mormon missionary in Honduras.

Omar still called for money; but, more often than not, the family could not afford to send him much even though the California economy and their own income appeared to be rising and stabilizing. He had seen photographs of Leticia and Yamileth and said that obviously they were doing well: they were fatter and whiter, which meant that they had enough food to eat and did not have to work outdoors. There had been some talk of his coming to Los Angeles, and in preparation he obtained his passport. The family briefly considered buying Omar a plane ticket to Tijuana on credit, and then somehow spiriting him across the border and maybe even finding a job for him in Yamileth's sweatshop, but that would still leave the question of Omar's adjustment to a culture far from his origins. Yamileth described life in Los Angeles as one of "run, run, run, to pay the rent, run to pay the expenses that are so big," and she and I both worried about Omar's ability to make that transition. How

---

[1]Interview with Tim Getten, in Estelí, July 1993.

would he adjust to working long days and driving on the freeways? Even Yamileth, as one of her nieces testified, never changed lanes.

In July 1993 a group of armed men attacked Estelí, putting the town back in the headlines for the first time since Somoza had bombed it years before. Yamileth called me, and we both searched frantically for up-to-date news. The attackers identified themselves as members of the Fuerzas Revolucionarias de Obreros y Campesinos (FROC, or Workers and Peasants Revolutionary Front), mostly former Sandinistas and some Contras who had united to protest the broken promises of the Chamorro government. Their demands included financing for farmers, access to health care, the creation of jobs, the nonprivatization of education—which would help Omar send his children to school—and the legalization of properties, including Yamileth's duplex, given out by the Sandinistas.[2] The attackers took over police stations, supermarkets, and the mayor's office. They cut communications, water, and electricity and also robbed the banks on the corner near where Omar lived. Government troops defeated the forces after three days of fighting in which fifty people were said to have been killed, one hundred injured, and many businesses and homes damaged. It was reported that "several bodies could be seen strewn about Estelí's downtown plaza. Buildings surrounding the plaza were pocked with shells, their windows shattered; and the charred remains of military and civilian jeeps and cars littered the streets."[3]

When the fighting was over, relatives reported that the roof of Yamileth's duplex had been damaged but that everyone was all right, with one exception: Omar had disappeared with the first shot. It was several days before we heard that the army, of which Omar had once been a proud member, had arrested and jailed him. For Sandinistas such as Omar, the slaughter was shocking, and an observer noted that "it was simply incomprehensible that Sandinista soldiers, who had once fought together against the Contras, were now killing each other"[4]—and, in Omar's case, imprisoning each other.

---

[2]CRIES/Nitlapán team, "The Armed Conflict in Estelí," *Envío* (Managua: Universidad Centroamericana, September 1993), 12:13.

[3]Tracy Wilkinson, "Nicaraguan Troops Dislodge Rebels; 150 Dead, Wounded," *Los Angeles Times*, July 23, 1993.

[4]Roger Burbach, "The Pot Boils Over," *NACLA Report on the Americas* 17 (January–February 1994), 7.

Omar was sent to a prison in Matagalpa because people in the neighborhood, members of the opposition party, had turned him in, accusing him of fighting against the same forces in which he had spent most of his life. According to the family, the charges were false. He had left Estelí when the fighting began—either out of fear brought on by posttraumatic stress syndrome or the suspicion that he would be arrested—and stayed with the family of one of Leticia's old boyfriends in the village of San Roque. When Omar was in the Ministry of the Interior, he had often worked for State Security, and the secrets he carried put his life in danger. Consequently, Irene determined that, for "political reasons," jail was not safe. After taking his case to a human rights organization, she arranged for his release, which took place a month or two later.

In late 1995, Omar's alcoholism and mental problems put him in a Managua hospital for several weeks. Now, when the family sends money to him, they send it in Irene's name, afraid that Omar will drink it up before he sets foot in the duplex. Yamileth has hired an Estelí lawyer because the owner of the land on which the duplex was built wants compensation, and she has arranged to pay the owner a few hundred dollars in installments.

The Family

In Los Angeles, the family lived in the South-Central house for several years. A block away the neighborhood deteriorated, but their street, snuggled up to the protective arm of the University of Southern California, felt safe. Early in 1995 they moved to an apartment located, almost literally, under the Santa Monica Freeway on a dreary semi-industrial street populated by Latinos in tiny houses or in pale pastel apartment buildings that proclaim "*Se Vende*" (For Sale) from banners. Although they felt safer out of the ethnic and racial mixture, they still did not know any of their neighbors in the apartment building, counter to the Nicaraguan tradition. The move was motivated by money: the house simply cost too much. Leticia and a daughter had earlier found their own room near the salon, but all the rest—numbering nine, ten, and sometimes more—lived in the four-bedroom, two-bath apartment. They missed the sense of being in a house, but the convenience of the extra bedrooms and bath made up for that. The front door remained open, as always, but Doña María would have found the overwhelming presence of pavement and freeway less than attractive.

Yamileth still had her fears, which she said had become habits, such as rarely wanting to leave the apartment at night. She vowed that other worries, such as riots, would not catch her unawares again. A year after the 1992 riots, as the second Rodney King trial ended in the conviction of the Los Angeles policemen, Yamileth kept the children home from school, stocked up on food, and no one left the house after four-thirty in the afternoon. The police, the gangs, and *la migra* were on the streets when the verdict came in. The López family was not. Another concern was that the INS was deporting Nicaraguans who had been granted asylum, at least on a selective basis,[5] but fortunately none of the family had asked for asylum because they firmly considered themselves economic, not political, refugees. Still, she worried. The January 1994 earthquake broke a living-room window and rattled their nerves, as did the 5.3 aftershock in March, which took place while I was interviewing her. We were seated at the kitchen table, and members of both of our families were in the living room. As the earthquake began, I numbly wondered why the window was rattling, but long before I understood that we were experiencing an earthquake, Yamileth had already bolted for the living room and Diana. Yamileth, still given to military-like descriptions, now calls earthquakes "the big enemy you can't hide from."

And then there were the gangs. The Pico-Union and MacArthur Park areas have more homicides than any other Los Angeles Police Department division. When a gang truce eroded in 1995, a fight took place near Leticia's salon. Sofía's husband saw it all and admitted as much when the police came. Afterward, Sofía tearfully yelled at him, "They'll kill us all, and it will be your fault!" Two days later, two bullets slammed into the salon, one breaking a window and the other embedding itself in the metal frame around the door. The family got the message.[6]

After the passage of Proposition 187, the members of Yamileth's family who were still undocumented stopped using any public hospitals or clinics; and, out of fear of deportation, they have not gone

---

[5]María Luisa Arredondo, "Nicas piden que no se les deporte," *La Opinión*, February 24, 1994.

[6]Street gang violence in Los Angeles County was considered an epidemic. Researchers documented the killing of 7,288 people from 1979 to 1994, amounting to 43 percent of all homicides in 1994, up from 18 percent in 1979. There are 1,142 street gangs and 150,000 gang members. Terence Monmany, "Medical Researchers Call Gang Killings 'Epidemic' in County," *Los Angeles Times*, October 4, 1995.

back. Yamileth pulled Nora out of school, explaining that her niece was afraid she would be turned in and *la migra* would take her away. "We live so far from the school that we worried that something could happen and she'd be gone without our knowing or being able to help. But the teachers called Nora and told her to come back, and she did."

More hardships were to follow. In August 1995 the authorities raided a sweatshop near Los Angeles that served as a virtual prison for Thai immigrants. A few weeks later, on a Friday afternoon and without giving advance notice, Yamileth's employers closed down their sweatshop, telling the forty employees that sales were poor. Yamileth, finding herself and Miguel suddenly without work, left hoping that they would eventually be called back and given employment once more. No doubt, the sweatshop sector, whose workers were estimated to number more than one hundred thousand and suspected to be overwhelmingly Mexican and Central American, felt the heat of the attention given to the Thai workers. Most Angelenos had somehow managed not to see the sweatshops in their neighborhoods where immigrants sewed "Made in the USA" on clothes. And I, who had once inadvertently stumbled into an Asian sweatshop in the Pico-Union district and who was known to decry the situation, was mostly saddened when Yamileth's shop closed down and put her in a perilous economic situation.

Seldom had we seen so much interest in immigration issues: initiatives popped up in other states, national leaders protested sweatshop conditions, the new border "czar" tightened up patrols between Mexico and the United States, politicians positioned themselves in front of flags and detailed the woes that immigration brought to the country, legislators increased penalties for forgers and employers, the INS commissioner vowed to institute a national computer identification system, candidates questioned the value of bilingual education, and policymakers proposed denying citizenship to children born in the United States to undocumented parents. All sides positioned themselves to look tough. Finally, and not surprisingly, the number of applicants for citizenship rose dramatically, especially in Southern California, which would eventually lead to an increase in Latino voters.[7]

---

[7]In California, one of the results of the wave of new citizens was to bring about a 40 percent increase in Latino voters, most of whom live in Los Angeles. Pablo Comesaña Amado, "Se espera un aumento del 40 por ciento de electores latinos en las elecciones," *La Opinión*, June 21, 1996.

Yamileth's family, many of whom were on their way to legal status by having married citizens or legal residents, worried less about *la migra* and more about the increasing gang violence. Yamileth saw it differently: the mobility of gangs was restricted by territories, but *la migra* could go exactly where it wanted to go. Nowhere was she completely safe, and the roundups seemed to be growing in number. Daily, when Yamileth left the house, she told Marisa to take care of her children if something were to happen. The "something" was being caught by *la migra* and deported. INS officials maintain that if they arrest an undocumented worker, such as Yamileth, in their sweeps, and if that person has a child who is a U.S. citizen, such as Diana, they will not remove that child from the schools and deport her. However, if Miguel, who is not a citizen, were still in school, he could be removed and deported, although this rarely happens because the INS would prefer to leave the child in the United States with a family member.[8] No matter what the INS said, because it still meant that Yamileth could end up being separated from her children, that terror always kept her on edge.

Her fears were not unfounded. As a result of actions taken after the disclosure of the Thai semi-slave sweatshop, the INS conducted roundups at other work sites and ran computer checks on workers' documents. Sweatshop charges abounded, making national headlines, touching some of the smallest shops in Los Angeles and some of the largest international ones. The Department of Labor revealed that more than 51 percent of Los Angeles sweatshops paid less than the minimum wage,[9] with some Los Angeles-area workers making as little as $3.10 per hour and working as many as fifty-five hours per week.[10]

Several months after its abrupt closing, the owners of Yamileth's sweatshop called the workers back; but she, as one of the most experienced employees and the one who trained others, had her wage lowered to the minimum. She did not complain, nor did she mention the lack of benefits and omission of timely notice of dismissal, or the unhealthy conditions. She took her allergy pills

---

[8]Lilian de la Torre, "INS continuará redadas contra indocumentados," ibid., May 2, 1996.

[9]Pablo Comesaña Amado, "Revelan abusos en la costura," ibid., May 4, 1996.

[10]The minimum wage at that time was $4.25. Stuart Silverstein and George White, "U.S. Rebukes Big Retailers on Clothing Sales," *Los Angeles Times*, May 21, 1996.

and went off to her job, with Miguel. Her good fortune was short-lived, though, because before long the computer checks reached her sweatshop. The "cones" continue to be made, but without Yamileth and Miguel.

The Past, the Present, and the Future

We all went out for breakfast together one Sunday morning—a large group taking up several tables in a Los Angeles coffee shop—and a stranger would not have known which children belonged to whom and would have noticed only that it was a handsome family, mostly Latinos with a few *gringos* thrown in, everyone prosperous look-ing, noisy, and happy. Middle age was starting to show on Yamileth's face and figure; out of respect for her age and position, her family deferred to her, and Manuel ordered her food from the English-speaking Vietnamese waitress. Diana, dressed in a blue denim jump-suit set off by a red blouse and red earrings, showed off fingernails she had painted bright red all by herself, like a little hairdresser in the making. Soon she would be a student in Head Start. Estelí, Nica-ragua, was far away.

We remembered Ken Bunker and his untimely death; Miguel, in particular, mourned his loss. The bakery had faded into family lore, even as the food section of the *Los Angeles Times* claimed that in some parts of Southern California, sweet pastries and breads from Central America are replacing the morning doughnut. The salon held the future. Los Angeles's Spanish-language newspaper, *La Opinión*, had featured an article on Latinos and the success of their small businesses. The accompanying photos showed the smil-ing faces of Marisa and Sofía, each cutting a client's hair, looking to all the world like winners. We also discussed how the passage of Proposition 187 had affected them; they said that life went on as it had before and they lived as they wished, but with a few more wor-ries. Of course, they had to keep Miguel from driving a car and running the risk of being caught again. It also, in their minds, elimi-nated the thought of Omar crossing the border; with the increased patrols, he most certainly would be caught. More significant, they knew that if they left the United States to visit Nicaragua, however briefly, they probably could not return unless they managed to ob-tain legal papers. Their choices, as those of other immigrants, have never been easy.

The family—albeit not in a so-called traditional grouping—is strong and united. Life has settled into a routine. Marisa cooks dinner on the weekdays, Yamileth on the weekend. Even though she still stews her pot of beans for her breakfast *gallo pinto*, the women dish up spaghetti or hamburgers in the evening. The same nieces who had once considered Yamileth a "parasite" now carefully look after her, and she them. Yamileth does not know if the change came about through her pregnancy, the bakery, time, or simply maturity, but she loves it now. She and Marisa are so close that they often have to hide their affection in front of Leticia.

While Yamileth works, Marisa takes Diana to the salon, where clients, mothers, aunts, cousins, and Grandmother Leticia watch out for all the children, passing them around as if they belong to everyone. When the fathers are present, they, too, are fathers to all. Occasionally, Diana calls her own mother *Tía* just as her cousins do, and Stephanie calls her father her own version of "Manuel" in imitation of her cousins. The family has equipped the back room with toys, a microwave oven, a television set, and space for the children to play.

In the apartment, Yamileth sleeps in a double bed with Diana, often Stephanie, and Marisa sometimes crawls in when Manuel works at night. Eddie, however, is not allowed to share this bed. Miguel stakes out the floor in a sleeping bag, and sometimes so does Nora. Yamileth likens herself to a mother hen, a *gallina*, who wants to protect her nieces' children and her own. When she sleeps, she still dreams of her own mother, who wonders why Yamileth left her alone or reminds her not to forget Omar.

After two attempts at passing the California drivers' exam, Yamileth now has a legal license. Manuel still works for Big John loading paper and plastic supplies onto trucks during the night shift, only now he is the supervisor. If Miguel one day obtains his legal documents, Manuel hopes that he can find a job for him at the same site. Marisa continues to grow into the role of the matriarch, the one that Yamileth and even Leticia depend on. Sofía works in the salon and takes her son with her every day. Chela, now a masseuse and an aerobics instructor, speaks unaccented English. Nora attends El Camino Real High School in Woodland Hills, a round-trip bus ride of two and one-half hours. She knows more about U.S. history than Nicaraguan and cannot see herself ever living in Nicaragua again.

Just as parts of the United States are becoming more Latino, many Latinos are becoming citizens and culturally part of the United States. A dramatic process is under way. The lines between our cultures are beginning to blur, as they are between Yamileth's life and mine. Through knowing each other, we are becoming more like each other, sometimes only in small, almost indecipherable ways. When I went south of the U.S. border, as have many before me, and when she later crossed the same border coming north, as have many before her, we brought our histories with us. Our culture, our civilization, our lives are somewhere in between all the vaporous borders, changing all the time and not recognized by boundaries. We met, and we were altered. Certainly not *la reconquista*. One culture? Not even that. But clearly we are both different from what we were before.

About the Author

Dianne Walta Hart grew up in Brookings, South Dakota, and earned degrees from the College of St. Catherine, St. Paul, Minnesota, and Oregon State University, Corvallis. In the 1960s she taught ninth-grade English in the Los Angeles Unified School District for five years, working two of those years in Northridge and three in the Watts area. Since 1982 she has been on the faculty at Oregon State University, where she is a senior instructor of Spanish. In addition, Hart serves as the Latin America Director of Global Graduates: The Oregon International Internship Program, part of the Oregon State System of Higher Education. She is the author of *Thanks to God and the Revolution: The Oral History of a Nicaraguan Family* (1990).

Latin American Silhouettes
Studies in History and Culture

William H. Beezley and
Judith Ewell
Editors

Volumes Published

Brian Loveman and Thomas M. Davies, Jr.,
eds., *The Politics of Antipolitics: The
Military in Latin America*, 3d ed.,
revised and updated (1996).
Cloth ISBN 0-8420-2609-6
Paper ISBN 0-8420-2611-8

Dianne Walta Hart, *Undocumented in L.A.:
An Immigrant's Story* (1997).
Cloth ISBN 0-8420-2648-7
Paper ISBN 0-8420-2649-5

William H. Beezley and Judith Ewell, eds.,
*The Human Tradition in Modern Latin
America* (1997). Cloth ISBN 0-8420-
2612-6   Paper ISBN 0-8420-2613-4

Donald F. Stevens, ed., *Based on a
True Story: Latin American History
at the Movies* (1997).
Cloth ISBN 0-8420-2582-0
Paper ISBN 0-8420-2781-5

Jaime E. Rodríguez O., ed., *The Origins of
Mexican National Politics, 1808–1847*
(1997). Paper ISBN 0-8420-2723-8

Che Guevara, *Guerrilla Warfare*, with revised
and updated introduction and case studies
by Brian Loveman and Thomas M.
Davies, Jr., 3d ed. (1997). Cloth ISBN 0-
8420-2677-0   Paper ISBN 0-8420-2678-9

Adrian A. Bantjes, *As If Jesus Walked on
Earth: Cardenismo, Sonora, and the
Mexican Revolution* (1998; rev. ed.,
2000). Cloth ISBN 0-8420-2653-3
Paper ISBN 0-8420-2751-3

A. Kim Clark, *The Redemptive Work: Railway
and Nation in Ecuador, 1895–1930*
(1998). Cloth ISBN 0-8420-2674-6
Paper ISBN 0-8420-5013-2

Louis A. Pérez, Jr., ed., *Impressions of Cuba
in the Nineteenth Century: The Travel
Diary of Joseph J. Dimock* (1998).
Cloth ISBN 0-8420-2657-6
Paper ISBN 0-8420-2658-4

June E. Hahner, ed., *Women through Women's
Eyes: Latin American Women in*

Nineteenth-Century Travel Accounts
(1998). Cloth ISBN 0-8420-2633-9
Paper ISBN 0-8420-2634-7

James P. Brennan, ed., *Peronism and Argentina*
(1998). ISBN 0-8420-2706-8

John Mason Hart, ed., *Border Crossings:
Mexican and Mexican-American Workers*
(1998). Cloth ISBN 0-8420-2716-5
Paper ISBN 0-8420-2717-3

Brian Loveman, *For la Patria: Politics and
the Armed Forces in Latin America*
(1999). Cloth ISBN 0-8420-2772-6 Paper
ISBN 0-8420-2773-4

Guy P. C. Thomson, with David G. LaFrance,
*Patriotism, Politics, and Popular
Liberalism in Nineteenth-Century
Mexico: Juan Francisco Lucas and the
Puebla Sierra* (1999).
ISBN 0-8420-2683-5

Robert Woodmansee Herr, in collaboration
with Richard Herr, *An American Family
in the Mexican Revolution* (1999).
ISBN 0-8420-2724-6

Juan Pedro Viqueira Albán, trans. Sonya
Lipsett-Rivera and Sergio Rivera Ayala,
*Propriety and Permissiveness in
Bourbon Mexico* (1999).
Cloth ISBN 0-8420-2466-2
Paper ISBN 0-8420-2467-0

Stephen R. Niblo, *Mexico in the 1940s:
Modernity, Politics, and Corruption* (1999).
Cloth ISBN 0-8420-2794-7
Paper (2001) ISBN 0-8420-2795-5

David E. Lorey, *The U.S.-Mexican Border
in the Twentieth Century* (1999).
Cloth ISBN 0-8420-2755-6
Paper ISBN 0-8420-2756-4

Joanne Hershfield and David R. Maciel, eds.,
*Mexico's Cinema: A Century of Films and
Filmmakers* (2000). Cloth ISBN 0-8420-
2681-9 Paper ISBN 0-8420-2682-7

Peter V. N. Henderson, *In the Absence of Don
Porfirio: Francisco León de la Barra*

and the Mexican Revolution (2000).
ISBN 0-8420-2774-2

Mark T. Gilderhus, *The Second Century: U.S.-Latin American Relations since 1889* (2000). Cloth ISBN 0-8420-2413-1
Paper ISBN 0-8420-2414-X

Catherine Moses, *Real Life in Castro's Cuba* (2000). Cloth ISBN 0-8420-2836-6
Paper ISBN 0-8420-2837-4

K. Lynn Stoner, ed./comp., with Luis Hipólito Serrano Pérez, *Cuban and Cuban-American Women: An Annotated Bibliography* (2000).
ISBN 0-8420-2643-6

Thomas D. Schoonover, *The French in Central America: Culture and Commerce, 1820–1930* (2000).
ISBN 0-8420-2792-0

Enrique C. Ochoa, *Feeding Mexico: The Political Uses of Food since 1910* (2000). Cloth ISBN 0-8420-2812-9
(2002) Paper ISBN 0-8420-2813-7

Thomas W. Walker and Ariel C. Armony, eds., *Repression, Resistance, and Democratic Transition in Central America* (2000). Cloth ISBN 0-8420-2766-1   Paper ISBN 0-8420-2768-8

William H. Beezley and David E. Lorey, eds., *¡Viva México! ¡Viva la Independencia! Celebrations of September 16* (2001).
Cloth ISBN 0-8420-2914-1
Paper ISBN 0-8420-2915-X

Jeffrey M. Pilcher, *Cantinflas and the Chaos of Mexican Modernity* (2001).
Cloth ISBN 0-8420-2769-6
Paper ISBN 0-8420-2771-8

Victor M. Uribe-Uran, ed., *State and Society in Spanish America during the Age of Revolution* (2001). Cloth ISBN 0-8420-2873-0   Paper ISBN 0-8420-2874-9

Andrew Grant Wood, *Revolution in the Street: Women, Workers, and Urban Protest in Veracruz, 1870–1927* (2001).
Cloth ISBN 0-8420-2879-X
(2002) Paper ISBN 0-8420-2880-3

Charles Bergquist, Ricardo Peñaranda, and Gonzalo Sánchez G., eds., *Violence in Colombia, 1990–2000: Waging War and Negotiating Peace* (2001).
Cloth ISBN 0-8420-2869-2
Paper ISBN 0-8420-2870-6

William Schell, Jr., *Integral Outsiders: The American Colony in Mexico City, 1876–1911* (2001). ISBN 0-8420-2838-2

John Lynch, *Argentine Caudillo: Juan Manuel de Rosas* (2001).
Cloth ISBN 0-8420-2897-8
Paper ISBN 0-8420-2898-6

Samuel Basch, M.D., ed. and trans. Fred D. Ullman, *Recollections of Mexico: The Last Ten Months of Maximilian's Empire* (2001). ISBN 0-8420-2962-1

David Sowell, *The Tale of Healer Miguel Perdomo Neira: Medicine, Ideologies, and Power in the Nineteenth-Century Andes* (2001).
Cloth ISBN 0-8420-2826-9
Paper ISBN 0-8420-2827-7

June E. Hahner, ed., *A Parisian in Brazil: The Travel Account of a Frenchwoman in Nineteenth-Century Rio de Janeiro* (2001). Cloth ISBN 0-8420-2854-4
Paper ISBN 0-8420-2855-2

Richard A. Warren, *Vagrants and Citizens: Politics and the Masses in Mexico City from Colony to Republic* (2001).
ISBN 0-8420-2964-8

Roderick J. Barman, *Princess Isabel of Brazil: Gender and Power in the Nineteenth Century* (2002).
Cloth ISBN 0-8420-2845-5
Paper ISBN 0-8420-2846-3

Stuart F. Voss, *Latin America in the Middle Period, 1750–1929* (2002).
Cloth ISBN 0-8420-5024-8
Paper ISBN 0-8420-5025-6

Lester D. Langley, *The Banana Wars: United States Intervention in the Caribbean, 1898–1934*, with new introduction (2002). Cloth ISBN 0-8420-5046-9   Paper ISBN 0-8420-5047-7

Mariano Ben Plotkin, *Mañana es San Perón: A Cultural History of Perón's Argentina* (2003). Cloth ISBN 0-8420-5028-0
Paper ISBN 0-8420-5029-9

Allen Gerlach, *Indians, Oil, and Politics: A Recent History of Ecuador* (2003).
Cloth ISBN 0-8420-5107-4
Paper ISBN 0-8420-5108-2

Karen Racine, *Francisco de Miranda: A Transatlantic Life in the Age of Revolution* (2003). Cloth ISBN 0-8420-2909-5   Paper ISBN 0-8420-2910-9

Christon I. Archer, ed., *The Birth of Modern Mexico, 1780–1824* (2003).
ISBN 0-8420-5126-0

David G. LaFrance, *Revolution in Mexico's Heartland: Politics, War, and State Building in Puebla, 1913–1920* (2003).
ISBN 0-8420-5136-8

9545